# CHEAT PLAY LIVE

# CHEAT PLAY LIVE

ONE WOMAN'S JOURNEY TO FEARLESSNESS
AND FREEDOM

LISA EDWARDS

REDWOOD TREE PUBLISHING

Cover design: Clare Baggaley

Publisher: Redwood Tree Publishing Ltd

ISBN (ebook): 978-1-7399340-0-2

ISBN (paperback): 978-1-7399340-1-9

 Created with Vellum

*For Mum, Dad ... and for Shubham, the only fish in my sea.*

# BEACHES

Wherever they are in the world, beaches are places where the universe speaks loudest; where earth, air, fire and water meet in their purest form. They broadcast a message we can only hear it if we let ourselves walk quietly in the light and listen.

## THE REDWOOD TREE

My father once told me a story about an old redwood tree—
how she stood tall and proud—her sprawling limbs clothed
in emerald green. With a smile, he described her as a mere
sapling, sheltered by her elders and basking in the safety of
the warm, dappled light. But as this tree grew taller, she
found herself at the mercy of the cruel wind and the vicious
rain. Together, they tore relentlessly at her pretty boughs,
until she felt as though her heart would split in two.

After a long, thoughtful pause, my father turned to me
and said, "My daughter, one day the same thing will happen
to you. And when that time comes, remember the redwood
tree. Do not worry about the cruel wind or the vicious rain
—but do as that tree did and just keep growing."

Lang Leav, *The Universe of Us*

# RHOSNEIGR BEACH

## ANGLESEY, NORTH WALES – 1974

THE WATER IS *shallow and warm and I'm holding my daddy's hand. I'm seven years old and I'm too old to be wearing just my knickers at the beach. My mum has forgotten my swimming costume, so I have no choice. There is a boy my age nearby and I feel embarrassed ... but then we spot creatures in the water and I'm distracted.*

*This morning, Daddy took me to the place with the longest name in the world: Llanfairpwllgwyngyllgogerychwyrndrobwllllantisiliogogogoch.*

*He walked with me along the station platform, next to the sign, and made me repeat every syllable in Welsh after him.*

*In the sea, now, we say them again.*

*Gogogoch. Gogogoch!*

*The sound of the words makes us laugh.*

*The light is so bright, reflecting off my feet in the water. There is no horizon, just endless shallow water and rippling sand.*

*There is only white light, a dancing light, and Daddy's hand.*

CHEAT

# NEW BRIGHTON BEACH

## NEW ZEALAND – DECEMBER 2002

IF YOU'RE SPENDING your honeymoon in a motorhome, driving around New Zealand, New Brighton Beach is a good place to start. It's not the most beautiful beach, but it's not far from Christchurch and you can reset your body clock after a long-haul flight. It's the perfect place to plan the weeks ahead in a local pub and wake up on your first morning for a romantic walk on the long beach and a coffee sitting in the dunes.

That is, of course, unless you've married the wrong man.

There were no rose petals or champagne breakfasts on our honeymoon. Instead, the two of us woke up in a motorhome bed, feeling wretched. Graham knew he'd gone too far and put his arm around my shoulders as we crested the dunes that backed the beach. He never did that normally – he said it made his arm hurt. We walked slowly, tentatively, filling up with sea air and promises to do better.

My new husband had been completely uninterested in the planning of our wedding and honeymoon. In a bar near the beach on our first evening in New Zealand, we spread out the maps, as we had done at home when planning other holidays. I traced the route we'd be taking, from Christchurch down to Queenstown and back up the west coast of South Island, staying in campsites.

Graham suddenly realised that this holiday involved lots of driving. For him. (I was a nervous driver and didn't really want to sit behind the wheel of a motorhome.) He shouted at me and made me cry. He'd had a stressful time at work with a toxic boss, but I'd steam-rollered through, making the wedding happen even though he wasn't ready for it.

There were suddenly rules to follow, motorhome rules that I didn't know were there until I broke them. I stacked plates the wrong way, stashed bags in the wrong places and put beds up in the wrong order. Graham was used to caravan holidays, so he knew how it all worked.

I already knew about Graham's 'house rules' because they'd been making themselves known to me in the new home we'd bought together two years previously. We'd moved from Brighton to a starter home in Bucking-hamshire when Graham got a new job there in 2000. He was extraordinarily good at DIY and I loved our starter-home project. We gutted the two-up, two-down terraced house and garden and made a place of our own. I tended new plants bought from the local garden centre and I couldn't wait to get home in the summer to deadhead them.

We loved to nest in our little home. We'd spend sun-drenched days in the garden: Graham pottering in his shed, grinning, holding a machete which he used to hack back the overgrown garden. We ordered pizza in the evenings, flopping in front of the TV, exhausted.

Our little house backed onto a poppy field where

Graham cycled and I ran. Sometimes we just sat and stared at it, me with a glass of wine in my hand.

I wasn't particularly practical in the home, so at first, I enjoyed having Graham's rules to follow. But then, after we completed the house renovation, they became a standing joke – the house rules you didn't know were there until you broke them. They ranged from stacking the dishwasher the wrong way to leaving the windows open at the wrong angle. And they reappeared again on our honeymoon.

As I drove the Maui along a road on South Island, bordered by glacial lakes and early-summer lupins, U2's 'Stuck in a Moment You Can't Get Out Of' came on the radio. I listened to the lyrics in stunned silence. Graham was sleeping through it – I'd agreed to help with the driving and I'd started to enjoy the 'alone' time on New Zealand's wide, empty roads.

We had the time of our lives, hiking, jetboating, driving around glorious South Island, fresh from its appearance in the second *Lord of the Rings* movie. The Maui motorhome was cosy, especially when it snowed in the New Zealand 'summer' at Milford Sound. We made coffee and ate Tim Tams in the queue of traffic into the fjord, watching 'cheeky kea' birds peck at our rear-view mirrors. We wore newly bought fleeces and waved smugly and warmly at other Maui drivers doing the same thing.

I befriended a pilot in Queenstown, Alfie, whom I called every day to check if the weather was clear enough for a helicopter trip. Finally it was, and later, I thanked Alfie for spoiling the rest of my life. Nothing would ever measure up to flying over Fjordland: the mountains, rivers and forests below us; me in the front seat holding on as Alfie swooped up waterfalls and skimmed over turquoise glacial lakes fringed with pink and purple lupins. Alfie took a picture of us standing above Milford Sound, smiling in our fleeces, nervously perching on a ridge. (We later found out that he was the camera pilot for all four *The Lord of the Rings* movies, when his name appeared on the credits.)

This was the holiday of a lifetime, but something was missing: a shared joy. My new husband appeared to be unimpressed by everything and seemed intent on comparing the landscape unfavourably to Scotland. Everywhere reminded him of his home country. He flew a saltire flag in the back of the motorhome to bond with his New Zealand countrymen: Scots that had migrated there in previous centuries. He was pleased when a worker on the path at Mount Cook said he must be Scottish, because he was wearing shorts to hike in horizontal hail.

On the way back home, via a beach stop in Fiji, I became obsessed with a couple who appeared to be wrapped around each other constantly; *how honeymooners ought to be*, I thought. We were not wrapped around each other. We were two people on an adventure holiday together.

As we bumped down on the tarmac at Heathrow, my new husband suddenly turned to me with the most joyful face he'd had in weeks and exclaimed, "That was the best holiday I've ever had!"

---

I went along with a Church of Scotland wedding for my husband's sake. And he was doing it for his mother's sake. It took place in a small Scottish castle that had been turned into a hotel. It turned out to have been the place where Graham's parents celebrated their own marriage, but his mother didn't mention it until our wedding day. I still can't work out why not: it was quite beautiful that we had chosen the same venue.

I stayed at the castle on my own the night before the wedding, observing the rule of not seeing my husband-to-be before the ceremony. While he had his best man and friends to stay at his mother's house, I stayed on my own in a huge dark room lined with books. It allegedly had a Grey Lady ghost and I was awake for most of the night, scared.

And deeply concerned that I was making a huge mistake.

I was absolutely determined to show how independent I was. I would stay by myself, get ready myself and walk down the aisle by myself. My parents were no longer alive and there was no one I wanted to walk me down the aisle. I had no bridesmaids and I had a blood-red wedding dress to further prove the point: I was determined not to be a regular bride. But I felt incredibly lonely. I really wanted someone to say, "Look, honey, this is all very well, but drop the act. Come and stay with us, you're family now."

In all honesty, I wanted Graham to stop me. But he was just going with the flow, like many men do when it comes to weddings – allowing his soon-to-be-wife to plan everything and then just turning up on the day.

My friends staying at the hotel didn't know where to look because there I was among them the next morning on my own. *The bride!! At breakfast!!* They didn't know what to say so they all left me on my own, in an exclusion zone. I needed a lift into the nearest town to get my hair done and eventually had to ask someone. They all assumed I was being looked after, but by whom?

To be fair, my mother-in-law did try and help me, sorting out flowers, the cake and a photographer. Plus, she made the most beautiful chocolates for each table. I even visited her on my own one weekend to sort things out. We didn't like each other very much, but we shared a brief moment of feeling like we were a normal daughter- and mother-in-law and I was grateful to her for it.

Later that day, I was about to walk into the room where Graham was waiting to marry me, but the minister was looking at me in panic. He appeared to have forgotten everything I'd told him about not having a traditional wedding. "What?! No one is walking with you down the aisle?!"

All my bravura rapidly diminished. I was wearing a red satin backless dress and a fur-collared jacket to marry someone I wasn't sure about, in front of a man resembling Jacob Rees-Mogg. "No, it's just me, as we discussed."

The minister tilted his head in resignation, sighed and walked through the doors into the room where we were getting married. I waited a moment before walking in behind him.

This was meant to be the ultimate show of independence. I was so proud, giving myself away, but inside, I desperately wanted the love and support of my parents, and the man I was marrying. Deep down, I knew that all this show – this backless red satin and bravura – was to make up for the lack of parents and the lack of love.

I knew this wedding was wrong. I knew it during the proposal, I knew it during the planning, and I knew it at that moment, as I was about to walk into a room in a Scottish castle full of friends and what was left of our families. Something had compelled me to ask this man to marry me, even though we didn't love each other enough. Something now compelled me to say, "I do."

I looked at Graham, suddenly serious and looking me straight in the eye. He stood confidently in his polished ghillie brogues. He was wearing his full regalia: kilt, sporran, clan socks and *sgian-dubh*. He was saying his vows, and I knew we were making a huge mistake. I said my vows anyway.

The castle staff played the wrong music. I wanted 'Myfanwy' by a Welsh male-voice choir, but suddenly Vivaldi's 'Winter' from *The Four Seasons* started playing. It was actually very appropriate for a gloriously frosty but sunny November day. It was all very *Four Weddings and a Funeral*.

Helen, one of my friends from university, read out a poem. I had chosen the classic Kahlil Gibran poem, 'On Marriage':

> *You were born together, and together you*
>     *shall be forevermore.*
> *You shall be together when the white wings*
>     *of death scatter your days.*
> *Ay, you shall be together even in the silent*
>     *memory of God.*
> *But let there be spaces in your togetherness,*
> *And let the winds of the heavens dance*
>     *between you.*
>
> *Love one another, but make not a bond of*
>     *love:*
> *Let it rather be a moving sea between the*
>     *shores of your souls.*
> *Fill each other's cup but drink not from*
>     *one cup.*
> *Give one another of your bread but eat not*
>     *from the same loaf.*

*Sing and dance together and be joyous, but*
    *let each one of you be alone,*
*Even as the strings of a lute are alone though*
    *they quiver with the same music.*

*Give your hearts, but not into each other's*
    *keeping.*
*For only the hand of Life can contain your*
    *hearts.*
*And stand together yet not too near together:*
*For the pillars of the temple stand apart,*
*And the oak tree and the cypress grow not in*
    *each other's shadow.*

I spotted some of the congregation looking confused. Weren't we supposed to be marrying each other, the very opposite of standing apart?

One friend knew I'd had cold feet and two weeks before the wedding, she'd told me to listen to that voice inside me. She knew that Graham had let me down during the biggest crisis of my life thus far and she told me I could still cancel – people would understand.

But I was invested in the wedding and a huge part of me wanted that moment in the spotlight in my red dress. I was thirty-five and I had developed a 'scarlet woman' persona. This version of myself was confident, glamorous, sexy and career-driven. She coloured her naturally chestnut-brown hair red and told everyone it was natural. She wore tight-fitting, sexy clothes while working in children's books, where most employees dressed modestly.

She did it to stand out and be noticed.

But she also did it to hide who she really was.

# BRIGHTON BEACH

## EAST SUSSEX, ENGLAND – 1995

Seaside towns are places where people go for liberation, for acceptance. The bright crystalline light bleaches out our flaws and allows us to come out of hiding, blinking into the sunshine. Brighton was the seaside town that liberated me, with its curved rows of white buildings reflecting the sun like a huge satellite dish.

This city by the sea is where people come to be seen and not seen. You can choose to be in full-colour against its bleached-white backdrop or blend in. You can try on any number of personas to see which one suits the new you. The city is full of eccentrics who distract everyone while you are changing.

---

Back home in North Wales, I'd been getting ready for a sixth-form Christmas-shopping trip to Manchester when I looked in the mirror and gasped. I reviewed my body in the cropped jumper (knitted by my mum), stretch jeans and tucka boots. I saw massive hips and thighs and immediately hated myself. How could I have not noticed how awful I looked? I look at pictures from that time and I feel sad because like most teenage girls, I was lovely. But tragically, I resolved to cover my body up in huge clothes because I thought it was so hideous.

Four years later, at university in London, I was a twenty-two-year-old 'mature' student with chronic body-image problems. I felt like a matron among the eighteen-year-olds in cinched-in Levi's, frolicking around the campus. I was fully used to shrouding myself in outsize clothes and hiding myself as much as possible from the world. It was the hardest thing to do on a dance course – I was required to be in front of a mirror for hours at a time. So, I wore huge T-shirts and baggy tracksuit bottoms and looked at myself as little as possible. I kept my head down, studied hard, avoided alcohol and barely spoke to boys.

And then I met Leon.

In 1992, I started work on the shop floor at Liberty in Regent Street because I needed to pay the rent. I'd tried my hardest to get a job in publishing straight after I graduated. I thought it was a done deal – I had a first-class degree in English and Dance and had launched a college arts magazine. Who wouldn't want me as an editorial assistant? But I was met by silence or rejection after every letter.

Everyone I worked with at Liberty was a graduate and we all thought of our jobs as just a stopgap before our real careers started. The store was like another campus, but this time I was determined to let loose. There was a pub next door to the store, The Clachan, that took every spare pound of my tiny salary. Once I joined the world of work, I joined the world of boozing and it was clear that new horizons opened up to me because of it. I was still wearing clothes that didn't fit me and actively repelling men, but at least I was doing it with a drink in my hand.

Leon worked in the Liberty warehouse. He was a six foot-seven Lithuanian and he would miraculously appear every time I had my break. We all went for peanut-butter toast in the tiny café opposite the store for our precious twenty minutes. I had started off by having a crush on his friend, a Yorkshireman who looked a bit like a miniature Timothy Dalton, but somehow I'd always be left alone in the café with this doe-eyed hulk.

Leon frightened me a bit, not least due to his considerable height, but mainly because he seemed so worldly and streetwise. Now I know that a love of Samuel Beckett and jazz are huge red flags but at the time, I was entranced. Leon listened to Arvo Pärt and read poetry. He wore a big military-style greatcoat and swished around London parks and pubs. He had haunted eyes and chiselled cheekbones. He was twenty-six.

The women I worked with commented on Leon during breaks. "He'd get it," they'd say.

I'd think, would he? What would he get? Would I give it to him? I wasn't sure I knew how to. I was twenty-four and still a virgin. The women teased me for obviously being in love – I couldn't eat anything in the canteen. But it wasn't love – it was nerves.

Leon started to stay over at mine and my body reacted to his touch as though he was testing my body for an electric current and finding it every time. But nights and nights passed where I would go to bed with him … in pyjama bottoms. I would allow him full access to my top half but my 'heavy bottom half' (as described by my ballet teacher) was off-limits and I felt paralysed by it. I lay there with him, stunned and overcome with desire night after night, as he stroked my breasts and kissed me. Me in my pyjama bottoms, my homemade chastity belt.

Leon was patient and took his time with me, but I knew I'd have to move things forward otherwise I'd lose him. We'd been seeing each other for about five weeks when eventually we arrived at The Moment. I remember staring into the mirror in my bathroom in Wimbledon and whispering, "Right – this is it. It's happening. Lisa, you're having sex. The pyjamas are coming off."

And then, when the moment came, he refused to wear a condom. I'd assumed he'd bring one and I didn't have one. I was just about prepared for a penis – finally – but definitely not an unsheathed one. He begged me to put it in, but I refused.

I remember it clearly – the outline of him above me in the darkness, begging to slide into me. I thought about all the women at work who'd 'give it' to him and here was me refusing. At least he didn't force himself into me against my will, but he was literally begging. I'd removed my pyjamas for nothing.

Not long after that night, Leon dumped me for being boring.

On Valentine's Night.

In bed.

Oh god, the frustration. I know I probably avoided more heartache and potentially a sexually transmitted disease or an unplanned pregnancy, but I wish I'd gone there when I was younger and able to make mistakes. Because it may have stopped me making even worse ones when I was older.

Damn those bloody pyjama bottoms.

After three years working in London, I found a job working part-time at Liberty in Brighton. I moved there to continue my studies at Sussex University but I only lasted eight weeks on the English MA course. Something was drawing me away from an academic life stuck in a dark library, and into the bright lights of Brighton.

The Liberty shop was on one of the narrow lanes near the pier and I walked there every day along the seafront from Kemptown (mainly because I couldn't afford the bus). I would work there, I decided, while I looked for that elusive job in publishing.

At Liberty, I met two women of my own age who were evidently living their best lives. I was so in awe of them: both blonde, red-lipped, wrapped in tight black clothes, wine and laughter. They must have looked at me and thought, what the hell is she doing here, in her huge clothes?

One night they took me clubbing and refused to let me go with them in one of my customary billowing outfits. I borrowed a fitted black dress from one of them ... and I can't quite remember what happened that night. All I know is that it was fun. What I do remember, though, is wearing a short skirt with black tights for work a few days later, as my body confidence grew.

I actually cried at the bus stop that morning. I cried because I was so afraid of what I looked like. Of looking stupid. Of looking ugly. It was another huge step forward in terms of my body confidence, but it took every ounce of courage I had.

Those women I worked with complimented and encouraged me. They had all the body confidence I lacked and I loved being around them. I lapped up their stories of their sexual exploits, living vicariously through them for a while, amazed at the way they threw themselves into the world. They owned flats, they drank wine, they had one-night stands and laughed about them afterwards. What was I doing??

Eventually I got a job in a publishing house in Hove. I'd looked up a list of local publishers in a business directory in Brighton library and walked into the biggest one in Hove to enquire about work. I was extremely lucky – they'd just bought another company and needed help unpacking boxes and doing the filing. I was paid £5 an hour to help the editors but it wasn't long before I started editing my own books. I realised that there were so many more open doors in publishing once you stepped outside London.

Instantly, my circle of friends widened. I moved into a flat with one of my colleagues and started to hit the town with her and her friends. I started to wear fitted tops, short skirts and black tights to work and liked how I looked. It became normal for me to show off my body in everyday life.

I met Graham in a club on the seafront. He was twenty-six and Scottish and we hit it off straight away. I went home with him 'for coffee'. I went home with him for my first full sexual encounter at the grand old age of twenty-eight.

I was struck by how beautiful he was. He'd been in a serious relationship which had ended five months before-hand. He'd hit the gym hard while he was recovering from the break-up. I remember him sitting in the open window of his bedroom, smoking after sex, the golden light of the streetlamp outside making him glow.

He was like an angel that night: strawberry blonde hair and golden, freckled skin, and a perfectly toned body. Everything, and I mean everything, was exactly as it should be. Not everyone gets a perfect first time, but I did.

I'm still not sure if he knew on that first night that I was a virgin. I used what I'd seen in movies to replicate the moves of an experienced woman, but I remember bleeding for a while after in his bathroom. But he was a perfect sexual match for me. His body seemed to fit me perfectly and I didn't feel any pain, physically or emotionally.

The next morning, in the kitchen with his housemates, I tried to laugh off the one-night-standness of it all by joking that he probably did this all the time. He looked at me sternly. "No, I do not," he said. We exchanged numbers and I walked home in a state of sexual grace.

But I was afraid, because it had taken so long to find him, that I'd never find anyone else again. I knew that I should continue to sow the oats I hadn't yet sown; that I should press the pause button on this guy; but I didn't. I had found something good – not quite as good as I'd hoped – but too good to turn down. After twenty-eight years of nothing – no boyfriends, no sex at all – here was someone I could see myself in a relationship with.

Later, Graham said he'd really meant for me to come back to his just for coffee. I discovered that his previous relationship had been a very serious one. He'd truly been in love. I didn't know how significant that was in a life because I'd never experienced it.

In retrospect, he wasn't ready for another relationship and I made it all happen. I was the one who called him four days after the one-night stand, and five years later I was the one who asked him to marry me. I often wonder what might have happened if I hadn't called him. He told me later that he was waiting a few days before calling me back. I was too eager to follow up.

When we moved into a flat in Hove together, I found the letters his previous girlfriend had sent him. They'd kept up a long-distance relationship for a few years and she had obviously been deeply in love too. They clearly enjoyed a very healthy sex life, even though they only saw each other once a month. I didn't recognise the Graham I read about in the letters.

The guy I knew seemed to prefer fixing the vintage car he had in his garage to spending time with me. I cried a lot in those early weeks, more out of sexual frustration than anything. The sex was good when it happened, but we weren't all over each other like I'd hoped we would be. I'd be left on my own in bed a lot, crying, and that never really changed throughout our thirteen years together. I reconciled it as how things were between men and women – I just had a lot of pent-up sexual frustration to satisfy after twenty-eight years of nothing. I also cried a lot because I went on the pill for the first time. I even had suicidal thoughts. It scared me so much I never went back on it – poor old Graham had to use condoms for our entire time together.

It seemed common in those days for women to be frustrated with their partners. In Brighton, my friends and I all sat round in bars after work bemoaning our partners' behaviour. It was the mid-nineties and the era of the lad and ladette. We played our part by pretending to be cool while the lads indulged themselves in infantile ways. We thought we were being the ultimate female companions, allowing the boys to do exactly what they wanted whilst we stood by, nonchalantly drinking pints of Stella. But in reality, we were – I was – just creating a world of festering resentment. (There is a reason why *Gone Girl* is such a huge publishing success – it captures that moment perfectly.)

At the time I thought all of us were Cool Girls with unappreciative boyfriends. It was only later that I realised that it was just me. Over time, I realised that my friends' partners stepped up for them when the chips were down ... when the bad stuff happened. Mine didn't.

Graham was affable, stable, kind and good-natured. Socially, everyone responded to him positively. But there was a lack of generosity there, and much as I didn't want him to play up to the Scottish stereotype, he did, especially in the way that he would stand by and let me pay for everything in bars and clubs. He would only ever have a few coins in his pocket when he met me in the pub after work. We called him 'Shrapnel Man'. Years later, I found out that he was holding on to the notes in his wallet, not wanting to break into them.

This pattern of withholding payment for things became a common theme in our lives together. He only seemed to have readily available money for trips with his friends: golf weekends or skiing trips. I called it the 'Bank of Boy' – and it was always open. But Graham would only ever go on holiday with me if I paid upfront for the flights and accommodation. He would then pay for everything once we were there, but he never matched the amounts I paid. At the time I didn't care. We were an adventure partnership.

As well as New Zealand, I drove through the Skeleton Coast in Namibia, the Icefields Parkway in Canada and Tsavo East National Park in Kenya with Graham. I now think of him as my adventure enabler – I would never have done any of those glorious things without him; I just had to pay for them.

In the first years of our relationship, I wasn't getting what I needed from Graham, and he clearly wasn't getting what he needed from me. He seemed more interested in the women gracing the covers of his *Loaded* magazines, piled high in the corner of his room. I knew I could never achieve that 'girl next door' look with honeyed skin and sunkissed hair that he seemed to like so much. Louise Redknapp, Denise Van Outen and Gail Porter seemed to be everything I could not be.

Graham withheld interest in me in the same way he held on to his banknotes. There was something held back in him when it came to celebrating anything – being happy with me, being happy for me. He withheld compliments saying my head might get too big, but I would look for – and eventually get them – elsewhere.

What he lacked, I later realised, was a generosity of spirit and crucially, he didn't really love me. I had proof that he'd had a very different relationship with his previous girl-friend, who was a successful lawyer. But he seemed to resent me for my professional success, jokily bemoaning my promotions in the noughties as a blow to his plan to make more money than me. I stopped trying to celebrate my success at home and increasingly went out to the pub with my work colleagues, who would buy me drinks and congrat-ulate me heartily on a promotion.

I look back now and realise that the late nineties were the point where my relationship with drinking started to change. Initially, I drank to lose my inhibitions, and later I drank to celebrate my professional success, after getting an editorial director job in London. I drank because I had to commute two hours each way to that job, and I drank to avoid going home to Hove and facing the reality that I was not in a true loving partnership. And when we did go out together, I drank pints of Stella that made me cry in the toilets of clubs by the sea, where I'd tell complete strangers how unhappy I was. It was fine, because it was the era of the Cool Girl, where we drank with the boys and thought we were exercising Girl Power.

I began to drink a couple of glasses of wine every day to

drown my sorrows. My mother had been officially diagnosed with dementia and I felt guilty at not being in North
Wales where my sister was attempting to tackle the situation. Mum was doing the classic dementia things like
leaving bubbling saucepans unattended and wandering
from the house. Pre-diagnosis, she'd got lost on a coach trip
back home after visiting me in Brighton. She was found
sitting patiently with her bag at a bus stop hundreds of
miles from Chester, where my sister was supposed to be
picking her up. It was the first big sign. Not long after, she
turned up at her neighbours' house ready to go to a wedding
that wasn't happening.

I was thirty-one and most of my friends still had their
parents, and even grandparents. They were having their
first babies. I wanted to live in their world – the world of the
living. I remember taking my mother out on that trip she
made to Brighton and I was embarrassed to be seen with her
on a bench on the seafront. She said strange things and I
didn't want my friends to hear them. My mother was like a
small bird by this point, clearly not eating enough, and I
didn't want anyone to see her frailty. I took her for a day out
in Lewes and had to take water and snacks with me in case
she needed them. I realised our roles had reversed and I was
looking after her.

After that visit, I remember being on the train home
from work, either dreaming of the chilled wine waiting for
me in the fridge at home or furtively drinking one of those
small bottles you can buy in train-station shops. It became
an everyday occurrence and I thought nothing of it. We all
did it, in publishing. Hell, the whole industry is fuelled on
wine and prosecco. My friends and I were like Bridget
Jones, working in publishing and our best relationship was
with a bottle of wine. We laughed it off and carried on doing

it. I didn't go beyond two glasses each night, but I needed it. I needed it to numb the pain of what was happening with my mother and escape from the reality of my home life.

I went home regularly to support my sister as she led the operation to get my mum the help she needed. First, we had to get her to agree to go to the doctor to be diagnosed, then she'd spend some time in hospital being assessed, and finally placed in care.

Let me tell you, there is nothing worse than doing this with your clever mother, who kept coming out of her brain fug to declare that she knew what we were doing and how angry she was. The doctor explained that this was how vascular dementia operated – like a shallow river, where most of the water ran smooth but every now and again, rocks broke the surface and caused ripples. She would have moments of extreme clarity, amongst the confusion.

Eventually, Mum was taken into Bodelwyddan Hospital in St Asaph, where I was born, for assessment. She had her own room, but the door would be left unlocked. When we visited her the first time, she was wearing someone else's cardigan.

The lounge area had a TV that was playing *Big Brother*. My mother thought I was Davina McCall. We all laughed. We laughed at everything because if we didn't, we'd cry. If we pointed out the mistakes my mother was making, she'd get confused and upset. Much better to laugh at it all, with her.

My clever mother.

My mother was finally placed into care just before the millennium. She thought it was a hotel, and regularly commented on the state of the rooms, the other guests and the service. It made us smile.

Elizabeth Pamela Mary Edwards was never quite happy living in a standard way. Her relationship with my father had elevated her in her early years as wife to a colonial civil servant in Kenya, complete with house servants. She wasn't good at being ordinary.

I remember my sister taking us out for a drive not long before she died, and my mother and I holding hands in the back seat of the car. I can still feel her hands – warm and sinewy, but soft.

I can still see her eyes the last time we saw each other. My sister orchestrated it so we were left alone. Maybe she knew the end was coming, and knew I needed to say goodbye.

During that last meeting, we talked about lipstick and my handbag. We used to enjoy shopping trips to Chester together and sit for hours having tea and cake, talking about clothes and makeup. "Smashing for the beach," she'd say, flicking through her many clothes catalogues in front of the electric fire at home, even though she barely visited a beach after her decade in Africa.

I saw myself appear in her eyes as we gazed at each other. Then it was over. I was Davina again.

When my mother died, I was staying with friends in Cambridgeshire for the weekend. Graham was with Helen's husband at a nearby military museum and I was with my friend, Helen, at a stately home when the news came through in a phone call from my sister. Mum had suffered a heart attack, my sister said, a big one. Her dementia had been caused by mini strokes – clots in her brain – and now the clots had stopped her heart too.

That afternoon, I tried my best to continue on as though

nothing had happened. I would not let this drag me down, I would carry on as normal. Helen looked at me for cues on how to behave, as I insisted on continuing our walk around the grounds of the stately home and going into the café for afternoon tea. I desperately wanted to stay in the land of the living for as long as I could.

You're probably waiting for me to tell you that Graham was there for me that day, when we drove to meet our partners at the museum. That he put his arms around me, comforted me and took control of things while I momentarily fell apart.

Instead, he pretended to be ill. He lay fake-moaning in the back of Helen's husband's car, clutching his stomach, looking for sympathy.

Helen and her husband looked on in horror. It was hideously embarrassing for me, because what he was doing was so obvious. But miraculously, within two hours, Graham managed to 'recover' enough to drive us both home.

I should have known – this was a theme that kept reappearing throughout our time together. I used to joke that he liked a game one-upmanship whenever I was ill. If I ever said I felt down, he was suddenly depressed; if I had a cold, he had the flu. And now he had what looked like gastroenteritis. I called it 'iller than you' syndrome.

Later in our lives, he got angry with me when I nearly drowned in the Thames near our home in Buckinghamshire, and completely ignored the fact that I was stuck in London during the July 2005 bombings. A pattern of not caring began to emerge and over the years, I silently stitched the pieces together.

That night, after Graham drove us both home to Hove, I went to a friend's house where she and her husband plied me with wine and sympathy. Graham didn't go with me for some reason – I can't remember why – but I remember crying drunken tears about his lack of support for me. I remember my friend saying she wouldn't be surprised if this ended the relationship, so I must have brought the subject up. I was crying partly because I'd lost my mother, but also because the man I'd chosen to share my life with had failed me epically in my hour of need.

I wish he'd sat me down and said, "I'm so sorry. I found it so hard to deal with what happened to you and I did pretend to be ill. I want to be there for you and make it up to you and I will do everything to help you in the best way I know – by offering practical help." But he didn't say anything. He did help me and my sister prep my mum's house before we put it on the market, but it wasn't enough. I knew I wasn't in a partnership when I walked down the aisle of the church alone, behind my mum's coffin. I knew this moment should have ended our relationship, but I didn't have the strength to leave.

In fact, in spite of all that, two years later, I asked Graham to marry me and offered him my own mother's tiny, worn engagement ring to put on my wedding finger. He sat on the edge of my bed, stunned by my offer. He said yes. In my defence, it was a leap year and I'd had a gin and tonic or two. After my mum died, my reliance on alcohol escalated in order to get me through the week. I needed to numb.

But why did I propose?! For one thing, I was approaching thirty-five and I didn't want to be an old bride. I felt a very real sense that life ended after that point – that you had to have everything sewn up. This rule existed in the ether, unspoken. Rewatching *Sex and the City* recently reminded me that we were all under the same impression in the nineties. Carrie Bradshaw was obsessed with what would happen to her at thirty-six. I guess it was something to do with the ticking of our biological clocks.

But I never did want children – something I decided at around fourteen, around the time I lost my Catholic faith. I'd never ever felt a maternal urge; not towards babies, anyway. I'd felt maternal towards dogs, or young friends and colleagues, but the last thing I wanted in my life was a small human. I didn't think they'd want me either – I valued my freedom too much. One thing was absolutely for sure: I knew that I could never be an older parent like mine (my dad was forty-eight when I was born, mum thirty-eight) because I couldn't put a child through the grief I was experiencing.

Graham and I had several conversations about not having children before we got married. He said that he was disappointed, but he'd rather be with me than have children with someone else. It was quite a statement, looking back, for a man to make to a woman. But I also wonder if he couldn't be bothered starting again with someone else and was just settling for me. I kept reminding Graham that 'never' meant never, not 'not right now'. I think on some level he was hoping I'd change my mind, but in my heart I knew I was not cut out for motherhood. I had a very strong sense that I was not in the world to do that.

And now I know that I wasn't in the world to be married, either.

# RHYL BEACH

## FLINTSHIRE, NORTH WALES – 1987

When I was twenty, I decided to kill myself. I stood on Rhyl beach, leaning against the railings looking out at the flat, grey sea with its flat, grey North Welsh sky. I felt the cold, damp air buffeting my cheeks. There was nothing worth living for.

Rhyl was the epicentre of eighties unemployment in North Wales. Its glorious Victorian past had faded to a grim present. Guest houses filled with people on benefits and hard drugs lined the seafront. The 'Suncentre' on the prom laughed in the face of the grey lid of North Welsh weather. It was the seafront of sadness.

I decided to kill myself because I'd been discovered doing something I shouldn't. This is something that has followed me round, even to this day. If I do something bad, I get found out, while other people get away with the same transgressions. It is the way of things. I was such a good girl at school, but for some reason I decided to drop a chocolate-bar wrapper out of the window next to me during English on day. A teacher walked past at that exact time.

Back in Wales before university, I'd been working part-time as a chambermaid in a local hotel to supplement my income. I was training as a ballet teacher in a local dance school. The hotel, which was more of a motel, was a place where I learned many of my domestic skills, my mother not being the greatest at those things herself. I still have Connie the supervisor to thank for teaching me how to clean a room properly, including vacuuming around the edges of a carpet and wiping a bath down after cleaning it, using a damp towel. She also taught me how to cook a breakfast and how to cope when you delivered anything to a room containing a naked businessman. Put the tray down without lifting your eyes and get out of there...

A well-meaning family member said I should not declare all my hours at the hotel to the benefit office. No one did, she said. So I declared half my hours, and the hotel dutifully declared all of them. The benefit office got in touch and demanded the repayment of everything I owed them and summoned me to a meeting in their offices in Rhyl.

I was utterly devastated. I didn't know at the time that this sort of thing was routine to the benefit office, who regularly hauled people in who were trying to cheat them out of extra money. My Good Catholic Girl self felt like a criminal.

My mother accompanied me to Rhyl on the bus and we sat on the sunless seafront in anticipation of the meeting, where I was given a simple telling off. I can honestly say that I felt my life was ending. At that time, I couldn't see anything but a grim future in front of me and I wanted to end it all. This was just the thing that tipped me over the edge.

Things were not good at home.

---

I was standing in the kitchen when my mother tearfully told me that Dad had gone to heaven. The angels were looking after him, she said, and I believed her. I was ten years old.

Up until that moment, in 1977, my Welsh childhood had been an idyllic one, filled with long, hot, drought-ridden summers and Christmases marked with big family gatherings and a sparkling, warm home. Wilf Edwards would be at the centre of it all, wearing his 'Head Barman' chain of office around his neck, jovially making sure everyone had what they needed.

I had been a 'mistake' – born eleven years after my brother and fifteen years after my sister – but I never felt like one. I was a loved child, especially by my daddy, who held me aloft on his shoulders and sang, 'Clap hands, Daddy comes, with a pocket full of plums!' He took me with him to the United Reformed chapel in Holywell where he played 'Little Brown Jug' or 'Surrey with the Fringe on Top' from *Oklahoma!* on the organ, just for me. My dad's mother, Dilys Myfanwy Edwards, had taken in laundry just to pay for his boyhood piano lessons.

Our house was filled with song. My mother had a beautiful soprano voice and was famous in our town for singing during the Second World War to keep people's spirits up. My dad often sat at the piano in our lounge, pulling out one of the Rodgers and Hammerstein songbooks and accompanying my mother on songs from *The Sound of Music* and *South Pacific*. They had been part of the Kenyan Operatic Society during their time in Africa, my mum singing and dancing and my dad leading the orchestra. (Paul Robeson, of *Show Boat* fame, attended one of their performances and I still have the signed programme.) I accompanied my Catholic mother to mass, and stood proudly beside her as she sang, "*Kyrie eleison!*" solo, high above the congregation.

And then, like a needle scratching across a record, everything went silent.

Some months before, I'd been waiting for my dad to come home after going to the pub and I'd found him hunched over the steering wheel of the car, feeling unwell. I knew something was very wrong but no one talked about it. And then suddenly he was in hospital and sending me handwritten letters on bright yellow notepaper. He looked like a man from Mars, he said, hooked up to lots of machines with wires.

When my father went into a hospice for terminally ill people, I had the choice of whether or not I wanted to visit him. When I did, he sat on the end of his bed wearing the Father's Day jumper I'd bought for him (well, my Mum had). It was a machine-knitted cream turtleneck with a brown geometric pattern on the front. It was from Man at C&A. I remember that he sat on the bed and made jokes to make me laugh. I'm sure he was wearing the jumper that time in the car too, but I don't trust my memory on that. He is always in that jumper in my mind.

I was scared by the old man in the bed next to my dad's. He looked like death, but my dad looked very much alive in his jumper. I remember the old man offering me candy twists from a small white paper bag on his sidetable, but I was too afraid to take one in case I caught whatever he had that made his cheeks hollow and his eyes water. I didn't like the smell of the hospice – it had that combination of bleach and boiled cabbage that reminded me of school dinners.

The night my dad died, I didn't visit him. My family

must have known he was going to go and didn't want me to witness it. I was happily playing with my best friend, Coreen, down the road and was spared the sight of my dad fading away. I wasn't even taken to his funeral.

But for weeks, months and even years afterwards, I kept seeing him everywhere: a man in his late fifties wearing glasses and a cream jumper. I'd stop breathing. I'd see him in my dreams, I'd see him on the street at home in North Wales. He was, and is, everywhere.

Daddy, my daddy.

I have a school picture taken around that time, just after he died. In it, I'm wearing my sister's hand-me-down floral dress, a green cardigan with a machine-knitted geometric pattern, and my long hair is in bunches tied with yellow panda bobbles. People who've seen it say I look like I have 'great depth', but what I had was experience of grief. The hollowness, the great weight on your chest – physically, I didn't know that grief manifested itself like a boulder strapped to your ribs.

Maybe some families pull together after loss like this and become a different but stronger force. Mine didn't. It fractured into small pieces. None of us were the same again.

My sister had moved out of the house by that point and was pursuing her own career, surrounding herself with friends who eventually became her new 'framily'. Over time, all of us became separate family units with friends who became our new framilies. Sometimes you can't go back and fix what is broken.

My brother and I continued to exist at home with my mother, who was experiencing an intense menopause. I think teenage kid and menopausal mum together in a house is a fairly common scenario, but I didn't realise what a heady mix it was at the time. All I know is that my mum was angry and miserable a lot of the time – something I put down to losing her soulmate, which was probably a big part of that mix. She never sang again after my dad died, except to teach me the sung prayers, '*Panis Angelicus*' (bread of heaven) and '*Ave Maria*'. She'd slowly removed herself from any sort of social life and was becoming a hermit.

I'd walk out of the house when she shouted at me for doing something good like cleaning the house, only to be picked up an hour later by my brother who scoured the Welsh countryside for a brooding teenager carrying her nightie in a bag on her back.

Wandering alone is something I did a lot after my dad died and in a way, I've never stopped. My teenage self roamed the hills around my Welsh home being buffeted by wild winds, looking for an endless horizon to stare wistfully over. My head was filled with Kate Bush and Emily Brontë and I looked for a Heathcliff to whisk me away on the back of his black steed. I was never going to find him in the rough on a golf course in North Wales, but I wore long, white, wafty dresses anyway, just in case, in which I ran after my Jack Russell, Sherry, when she went off chasing sheep.

A therapist later told me how important freedom was to me. I hadn't known it consciously, but after she said it, I realised how true it was. It manifested in lots of ways, not least wandering about alone on a Welsh moor. Two decades later, I began to run obsessively. I ran further and further away from the marital home. Looking back, I can see myself on an escape mission, one run at a time. I had started what would be a ten-year stint of low-carb dieting and lost a lot of weight. Running kept the weight off, but it also kept me out of the house where I would have to face the reality of my situation.

For one thing, I was running away from being a housewife. For some reason, I felt duty-bound to iron Graham's shirts and cook his meals. If I didn't, he went to work in wrinkled shirts and ate bad food and I couldn't bear it. With no discussion whatsoever, I found myself sliding into the housewifely role his mother had previously inhabited. It was my role to clean the inside of the house whilst he looked after the outside of it.

He came from a family with a strong work ethic, and they viewed household and garden chores as the most important way to spend time outside paid work. I had grown up with a mother who had never had any interest in housekeeping or cooking. Like me, I think she knew it was a thankless task and she would end up shackled to the home when she'd rather be outside it. (I also think she may have preferred to have remained childfree and lived her own life, but I'll never know the answer to that.) I remember her forcing my dad to take us all out for a 'run' in the Austin Maxi to places like Llanrwst in Snowdonia or Ruthin Castle for tea on a Sunday.

In my late thirties, I ran away from the house and its chores, and during the week, I stayed out later and later after work. I had become a successful publisher and Graham was less and less happy to celebrate it with me as my salary moved further ahead of his. I was managing a list with major successes in every category of children's publishing and was part of a dream team of people leading the business. I felt valued and energised.

This was the sort of success that only occurs once in your career in publishing, if you're lucky. Our books dominated the book charts and were being made into movies and TV shows. My life revolved around book-fair parties and red-carpet events. I knew that there was only one chance to enjoy it all and I went for it. I made the most of every moment and kept silent about it at home.

During that time, Graham started offering to come and pick me up from the train station when I was running late (which was every day) but this act of uncharacteristic generosity lasted about five seconds in my head before I realised what it really was: a way of getting me home quicker to cook his dinner.

---

We lived in a small, damp, pebble-dashed bungalow on a hill outside Holywell in North Wales. We'd had to move out of a much bigger house in the town after my dad died and my mum's finances didn't stack up. She couldn't afford to put central heating in so we had to rely on electric heaters, and later storage heaters, in each room.

Other people living in the little estate on the hilly moorland above our town, Holywell, had clean, neat, dry, warm bungalows. But ours was filled with sadness. It revealed itself as a black damp climbing the walls, which were nicotine-stained from the smoking my mother insisted on doing with all the windows closed. We huddled around the electric fire in the lounge, and I gave myself chilblains from roasting my feet in front of the fan heater in my bedroom.

None of us had any money. My mother was existing on a widow's pension and a small donation from the Masonic lodge my dad had belonged to. I was claiming benefits while I was teaching ballet and earning cash from the hotel; my brother was in a similar state to me. All of us snipped at each other about money, especially about how much petrol to put in the car (we could afford £5 at a time). We existed on a diet of canned food, yoghurt, biscuits, ginger cake and malt loaf supplied by my mother. We had roast chicken on Sundays.

I lived in fear of anyone visiting the house. The smell of it would greet them at the door – a mixture of nicotine and damp. At high school, my 'best friend' told everyone I stank. I did. We did our washing at home and it barely dried in the dampness. I did smell. And I hated it. I wanted to feel fresh, warm and dry. That friend dumped me because I stank and I couldn't afford to go to gigs with her. She simply exchanged me for wealthier, sweeter-smelling friends.

During my late teens, only two friends managed to cross the threshold of my home and I still cringe thinking about it. My oldest friend, Coreen, one of the most wonderful people you will ever meet, visited every week, and she continued even when I wasn't there, to keep an eye on my mum. I'll never forget her kindness.

In retrospect, all three of us living in that grim little bungalow were struggling with life. Even before benefit-gate, I started to get black thoughts about removing myself from the world and went to see the doctor. He handed me tissues as I blubbed in front of him, and he followed up with a prescription for antidepressants. I remember walking around like a zombie, just staring out into the world, not engaging with anything except my ballet-teaching.

And then, after benefit-gate, I couldn't think of a reason to carry on living. I'd done something that might seem fairly tame now, but at the time it made me feel like I couldn't live with myself. I had the bottle of pills on my bedside table and I thought I would take them and simply lie down and go to sleep.

I remember saying goodnight to my mother and brother as I did normally, thinking it would be for the last time. I knew I should probably drink some alcohol to make the pills more effective, but we didn't have any and I figured a lot of pills would do. I don't think I wrote a note – but maybe I've erased it from my mind. I lay down to sleep for one final time...

...and woke up with my mother standing above me, and her brother, my uncle, behind her. I was extremely drowsy and the two of them were trying to rouse me to go the ballet class I was due to teach in Rhyl later that afternoon. No one spoke, ever, about what I'd just done. They simply bull-dozed over it with 'let's get on with the day as though nothing happened' energy. I did get up and I did teach, in a complete daze.

But after this attempt, something lit up in my brain. I got a new zest for life. I got a job in the Liberty shop in Chester and was still teaching ballet, but my world began to expand. I rented a house with a work colleague in Chester for a year and got a taste for freedom. I was twenty-two and I knew I had to go to university; my brain was willing it to be so.

I'd stayed in my hometown and planned to teach ballet for the rest of my life but suddenly it wasn't enough. When she found out what I'd decided to do, my ballet teacher cried, "If I'd known you were clever, I'd have told you to go years ago!"

I chose a Dance and English degree at Roehampton University in West London and in autumn 1989, my brother drove me down south. I didn't stop crying for three days after he left me in my student dormitory, but I'd got there and I wasn't going back.

It's funny – my mother used to say that there was always a time in your life when it was right to do something and it wasn't always when you were 'supposed' to do it. She was right. I'm glad I went to university when I was ready because I did really well academically, even if I failed to explore everything else that people usually do at college.

My mother revelled in my academic success because the Second World War had got in the way of her own ambitions. She was clever, which resulted in her being great at cryptic crosswords, and annoyingly answering all the questions on *Mastermind* and *University Challenge* correctly. I phoned her every time I got an A* for an essay, which began with the first one, and I was determined not to let that standard slip. For her.

I knew I was starting to live the life she wished she had led, although she never said anything. She sent me little floral cards in the post with simple *'Love Mum x'* messages inside, just like the ones she'd pushed into my lunchboxes on school trips back in Wales. I've still got them.

I kept my home visits to a minimum. In my new student single room, I finally had a clean, warm, dry place to call home. I didn't smell funny. My clothes were washed in a machine. I didn't take ages to go to sleep because of the smell of nicotine in my nostrils. I would happily have guests round to my room.

When I did go home during the holidays, I pretended I had to return early for some reason. I went to bed early and counted down the hours until I could leave. I kept my belongings tightly zipped up in bags so they wouldn't smell of damp or nicotine. But they did, when I poured them back out onto my bed back in London. They smelt of sadness.

My mother had always told me to 'keep my hand on my ha'penny' and so I did, avoiding any real contact with boys for the whole three years at university and resisting the lure of alcohol. I wanted to be in control of my ha'penny at all times. I often wonder what would have happened if I'd just let myself go.

There was one moment where I did, just briefly. One night during those first weeks, I was surprised to find Chris, a gorgeous sport studies student, flirting with me at the college bar. He had floppy hair and a laddish grin. I let him put his arms around me on the way back to our rooms, and he took me to a dark chapel that was part of the campus. He pulled me to him, kissing me softly. I couldn't believe it was happening to me (and later I concluded that someone must have put him up to the 'challenge'). I kept my hand on my ha'penny, thinking there'd be another chance to take things further, but I didn't know that you had to seize the moment. I'd only had one kiss before Chris, and that was when I was around fourteen.

I wore my hair in an absurd variant of the eighties' mullet – short on top with a long plait draped down my chest – trying to look like a Thompson Twin. (I wasn't brave enough to cut the whole length off so I just had the top cut and wore the rest in a plait – most of my teen years were spent growing out that mad top layer of hair.) At a rugby club disco, I surprised myself and everyone else by catching the eye of a guy with an equally absurd Flock of Seagulls crest. We were sitting adjacent to one another on seats facing the opposite way. He leant back, I leant back until we could lean no more without falling over. Eventually we turned and snogged one another's faces off. We didn't speak and I didn't even ask his name at the end. We simply turned back to the friends we were with and went on with our nights. It was brilliant.

The next day at school everyone was in shock. Lisa, the 'immaculate conception' had snogged someone.

When I asked Chris the next day if we were going to see each other again, he blanked me in front of everyone. It seemed that in only a matter of hours he was going out with a girl who knew how to seize the moment.

I just wasn't that girl.

# CHINA BEACH

ON CHINA BEACH near San Francisco, I found an open Californian mussel shell, lying on a rock, its insides prismic, with an unexpected peacock-blue iridescence. Both halves of it lay open to the sky, as though it had come to the beach to sunbathe naked and hadn't intended anyone else to witness it. I took a picture of it. On the outside it was sea-worn and unremarkable, but on the inside it gleamed like a jewel.

My friend, Elv, remarked on how special it was, lying there, waiting to be found and cherished.

*Like me*, I thought.

I sat on the stretch of sand, watching my friends swimming and gazing over towards the Golden Gate bridge and the hills of Marin County. I laid my forehead on my drawn-up knees and felt sad. My friends were worried, but I needed to sit with the feeling and think about my options.

Out of the blue, a work colleague, Katherine, had offered Elv and me the chance to join her on a trip to San Francisco, where she'd be visiting her family. We couldn't believe that management gave us the same time off together

– we were all editorial directors in the publishing company we worked for.

Katherine gave me a copy of *Eat Pray Love* by Elizabeth Gilbert at the airport on the flight out. At first, I wasn't buying its religious undertones and *'this book will change your life'* copylines, but I finished it before we landed. Here was a woman singing my life with her words: married to a good guy, nice job, nice house, nice life. But she needed more, and she broke away to get it.

Five years after my wedding, I knew I had to break away from Graham and Katherine and Elv both knew it too. I spent the week with them locked in contemplation, drinking Sonoma wine, exploring the redwood tree-filled area around our villa in Russian River. It was the first time that I'd gone on holiday without my husband since we'd met. I'd tried to make out that my keenness to go on the trip was purely for the travel experience, but I knew that I was really going to see if I could reconnect with another man.

I met David on a work trip in 2006. It had come about because one of the books I'd published was made into a movie and I'd been sent to Cannes with the movie company, for their 40th birthday party. I was thirty-nine.

It was a warm spring evening in the south of France and I walked up the red carpet into the party feeling fantastic. I'd lost at least two stones from dieting and running and I was wearing a Mediterranean-blue halterneck maxi dress and sparkling diamond earrings loaned from a friend. I was at a party at Villa Rothschild thrown by a major movie company, and I was drinking champagne among ice sculptures on a warm May evening. I knew it would be a career highlight even before it started.

I joined a group of guys I knew from a videogame company and we explored the villa's gardens and danced to the DJ's songs. He was an early-days Mark Ronson, who had a cigarette hanging out of his mouth as he nonchalantly changed tracks. He played 'Valerie' by Amy Winehouse – he'd just produced her debut album.

David approached me with a northern accent and a big grin. He was from Manchester. He was four years younger than me, but we were captivated by each other. David told me he usually went for younger women but there we were, dancing and laughing in the open air, holding glasses of chilled champagne, while the warm night swilled around us.

We went back to our hotel with the rest of the group, but the party dissipated after an attempt at skinny-dipping in the pool was thwarted by hotel staff. I followed David to his room and we had drinks on his balcony. My body ached for him to touch me, but I knew I'd have to go back to my room and have a word with myself about the ring on my finger.

As we leant on his balcony holding drinks from his minibar, he told me he had a girlfriend back home in the US – in San Francisco.

I excused myself at around 4am and made for the door – I had a plane to catch in the morning and would be leaving in a few hours for the airport. We hugged, but the hug refused to end.

And oh, how I fantasised over and over about what happened next. It was so beautiful, so erotic, so like a movie version of my life.

He simply moved his hand from the small of my back

and began to draw his fingers softly up my shoulder blade. It was the tenderest touch I'd ever felt and I groaned. His hand found its way to my neck and into my hair as he kissed me. He kissed my lips, my neck, my shoulder...

There had never been a moment or a kiss quite like it.

Nothing more than those kisses happened, but it was as seismic as full sex as far as my life was concerned. More so, perhaps.

I returned to the UK, and David to the west of coast of the US, but there was a crackling current of electricity between us that lasted for months, even years, after.

I look back and acknowledge that this was an act of adultery even though sex wasn't involved. At the time, I convinced myself that the massive geographical chasm between us was stopping me from tipping over into actual commandment-breaking.

The first time David texted, I was in the middle of a meeting at work. My Blackberry buzzed on the table. *"Do you still think about that night?"*

My heart leapt as I read the words. *"God yes. All the time,"* I responded.

I couldn't wait until the meeting ended to continue the conversation. My heart was racing and I couldn't follow what was going on. I'd spent hours fantasising about what might have happened with David that night and I wanted to hear his version.

We began to sext at a time before sexting had been invented. Sometimes I'd be at my desk when he messaged me, sometimes out for a run in the countryside. Sometimes I'd be on the train, squirming in my seat. The world seemed to slow down as our imaginations ran riot. I was living on the electric eroticism of his words.

*"I'd like to watch you be fucked by another man,"* he told me one day. *"Really fucked hard."*

No one had said those words to me before. I found words I'd never uttered to respond to them.

We were driving each other wild with desire and I lived off the energy we were generating. I remember my husband saying to me, just after Cannes, that he thought I was having an affair. He was laughing as he said it, and so was I as I denied it, but to all intents and purposes, I was. It was an affair by text and my husband was asking me to tell him the truth, but I didn't.

I wanted the excitement, the thrill of my secret world, and it had woken up something deep inside me. Desire. David was someone I could test it out on with relatively little risk. He wasn't even in the same country and it wasn't physical, after that first encounter. It was word-based, and I could access it at any hour via my Blackberry.

I often wonder what I'd have ended up doing if Blackberries and then smartphones hadn't existed – there is no doubt that technology enabled me to explore a life beyond my marriage, to test the waters on the other side. I had spent hours of my life up until this point, at restaurant tables, bars and outside airports, waiting for my husband to finish a cigarette. Now I couldn't wait for him to go for one so I could access the secret world via the device in my pocket. It was like being in a virtual universe where I was desired by a man, unlike the real one I was in, where lawn-mowing was preferable to having sex.

But when I arrived in San Francisco, David lied to me about his whereabouts. He was in London, he said, but I discovered later that he'd been in California the entire time and just lied to avoid meeting me. I'd often receive messages from David in the early mornings, because of the time difference, usually after he'd been out drinking. It took me months to realise that he was a serial drunk-texter and that there was a world of difference between Daytime David and Nighttime David.

But even without David, that trip to San Francisco sealed my fate.

---

Just like the author of *Eat Pray Love*, Elizabeth Gilbert, I was with a man whom many women would consider the perfect life partner: good-looking, good-humoured, good job and good at DIY, and here I was contemplating leaving it all behind. I didn't want the home-based life Graham was offering, but I knew many women would. I had no doubt that, like many men, he would find a partner within minutes of me leaving him. I had to think very carefully before letting all of that go.

I didn't have a moment crying in existential agony on the bathroom floor as Liz Gilbert had, but somehow my San Francisco holiday gave me the time and space I needed to think about what I wanted to do. I decided I would test the water outside my marriage; not virtually, but physically, in real life.

I wanted to see if the grass was actually greener on the other side. David had made me think it might be, but I couldn't be sure. What if that was a one-off? After all, the one guy who'd shown me any interest had pretended to be on a different continent when I turned up on his Californian doorstep. I could potentially be giving up my Mr Nice Guy for nothing.

But deep down, I knew. I'd known for a long time that Graham and I weren't meant to be together, almost since the very beginning. I was wasting my life (and his) on a mismatched marriage. We even had a joke for it, which we'd adopted from another couple who used to say it to each other in jest: "We're locked in a loveless marriage!" The trouble was, we actually were.

For a while the whole idea stayed in my head, and then, quite unexpectedly, I got a lead. I was at the hairdressers and I was reading a piece in a magazine featuring a dating website for married people: it was called Illicit Encounters. I read it feverishly, hiding the page from the person doing my hair. My heart beat faster. I didn't know about this option. I memorised the name of the site and planned to look it up as soon as I could on my home computer, the iMac I'd bought with my first work bonus. I was so scared of even searching for the website at home – it was massively risky because although the computer was mine, Graham had set everything up so that it was shared between us with two different logins.

In a way, the risk was its own endorphin rush. My heart raced at the thought that Graham would be able to check the search history, and whilst I became adept at clearing every trace of my activity on there, I think a very subconscious part of me wanted to be caught. The path I was laying was so obvious and traceable to anyone remotely interested in my life. But he wasn't, so I got away with it.

I set up an Illicit Encounters (or IE as users call it) profile while Graham was out one day. No picture, just an image from my photo library that I thought summed me up. It was the mussel shell washed up on that San Francisco beach, its two halves tentatively opening to the sea air. *Here I am*, it said, *waiting to be found and cherished.*

The matches started to come through and it was incredibly exciting. It didn't seem to matter that I didn't have a proper profile picture. These guys registered their interest anyway. I started to chat to a few. They were bored and looking for excitement, they said, not necessarily a way out of their marriages.

I had to wait a long time between opportunities to log on, so I began to take risks like looking up the site at work after hours or loading the dating-site app onto my Black-Berry. I spent my hours commuting to and from work, reviewing profiles and chatting to these men.

The first guy I met up with was Patrick. He was sitting outside a wine bar grinning at me when I arrived at the designated hour. He had floppy Hugh Grant hair and wore a light-pink shirt and cream trousers. He was tall and intimidating, despite the grin and the fast-flowing jokes. He was also older than me, but I never found out how much. Whatever his age, he looked good for it.

I was scared. Scared of this man who was so different to Graham. Scared of what he might do with me. Scared of what I might do after a few drinks. So I drank to find out what would happen.

What happened was that we talked and laughed and had an intelligent, flirty conversation. The sun went down as we sat outside the bar, agreeing to have another bottle of wine.

I revelled in it, this man's attention, his obvious enjoyment in my company, the lovely wine. I felt sexy and powerful in my wrap dress. This was on a whole other level to anything I'd ever experienced with a man. I felt desired. I felt equal and respected. And I even felt equal and respected when he suggested that I accompany him to his office which was conveniently round the corner from the bar. It was closed but he had the key.

Halfway there, I halted and I told him I was scared. He

told me that he wasn't going to make me do anything I didn't want to do – I was free to go if I chose. I was in fight-or-flight mode – I simultaneously wanted to stay, and I wanted to go home to Graham. This was meant to be a drinks date, not a sleepover.

Patrick exuded danger, despite his Hugh Grant hair and well-educated wit – perhaps he was the Heathcliff I'd been longing for since I was a teenager. I clung on to his desk, dress pulled up round my waist, being rammed hard and crying out with every thrust, laughing with joy and fear. He grabbed my hair and pulled it back, asking me if I liked it.

Yes.

Yes, I did.

I went home that night, late, suddenly alive in the world.

I could feel my heartbeat, and the place where Patrick had been inside me.

I slipped into bed next to my husband.

*Sing for absolution*
*I will be singing*
*Falling from your grace*
*There's nowhere left to hide*
*In no one to confide*
*The truth runs deep inside*
*And will never die*

I played Muse's 'Sing for Absolution' relentlessly on my iPod for an entire week. I knew that my behaviour was wrong and that innocent spouses were getting hurt, but I did it anyway. The transgression powered on, fuelled by me finally getting the attention from a man that I thought I deserved.

I had no excuses for how I acted then and I still don't. I don't regret taking action, but I regret that I did it while I was still with my husband and that I did it with married men. Catholic guilt and shame raged inside me at the same time as the fire of my sexual freedom. To assuage my guilt, listening to Muse on repeat became my internal confessional booth.

I agreed to meet Patrick again a week later for drinks and dinner. This time he'd booked a room at his club. I hadn't intended to stay over so I phoned my husband to say I'd be staying with a friend following late work drinks.

I loved the evening Patrick and I spent together. We met in a lovely central London restaurant and spent the evening drinking wine, eating lovely food and having intelligent conversation.

That was the thing about Patrick – he was smart and seemed to like me for my intelligence as well as the sex. Our conversation was actually foreplay – a chance for both of us to have a no-strings chat with someone who was interested in what the other had to say. My husband and I would go out for dinner and I'd struggle to keep the conversation going in between his cigarette breaks.

As a younger woman I'd fantasised about finding a 'coffee-shop' boyfriend, with whom I'd spend hours talking about this and that. But I'd got a man who'd gulp down his coffee in five seconds flat and want to leave the coffee shop straight away because he'd finished his drink. What was the point of lingering? he'd ask. Finally, here was a man who wanted to linger.

And the sex. I had found a man who wanted sex with

me three times a night or more. I'd stopped initiating sex at home because of the inevitable rejection I'd receive, so it relied on Graham suggesting it, usually after he'd finished his morning chores at the weekend. I was way down the priority list and allotted an afternoon time slot. We called it Afternoon Delight, but really it was sex when he was ready for it. And although it was always good, it was never enough for me. It was polite and gentle.

There was nothing polite or gentle about Patrick in bed. He had the power to scare me. Even his body scared me. It was so different to my husband's in every way – taller, leaner, broader-shouldered, longer-legged and with a large cock and balls. He was ex-military and had that 'ready for anything' taut musculature about him. All of him scared me because I was so used to my husband's 'perfect fit for me' body. Nothing scared me about Graham and perhaps I needed to be scared.

I remember the next morning so vividly. Patrick ran me a bath and I remember thinking how sweet it was, that gesture, after the night's roughness. He made me feel relaxed and comfortable, and above all, beautiful. He wasn't holding back on compliments, and I drank them up thirstily.

I called in sick to work – another big transgression for me – and walked to John Lewis on Oxford Street to contemplate what I was doing. I felt guilty but at the same time, I thought I was getting what was due to me after years of deprivation. For some reason the John Lewis café felt like a safe space to contemplate it all. Maybe it was a church I could say a few Hail Marys in and find myself absolved of all sin.

There would be a few heart-stopping moments when both of our phone bills arrived on the doormat in Graham's name. Happily, his interest in the post was even lower than his interest in me, so I always got there first and ripped up the pages and pages of texts to David, Patrick and the guys that came later. Thank goodness he opted for paper bills and not e-statements that could be emailed to him.

Everything was working in my favour – and proved that either Graham knew what was happening and buried his head in the sand, or he was completely uninterested. Maybe a bit of both. If he did suspect anything, he never showed it beyond the post-Cannes moment. I was able to hide and destroy all evidence and I was never questioned about any of it. It was all too easy to get away with ... and that was a disappointment in itself.

But my husband was, in spite of his attitude towards me, a good man who deserved better – a better life, perhaps involving children, and a nest-building wife who would appreciate his lawn-mowing skills. He shouldn't have been with a woman who treated him like I did.

I knew that I would take more and more risks with IE and eventually I'd get caught and really hurt him. Finally, after several months of 'encounters', I resolved to leave him.

And I made a pact with myself not to see any more married men.

# WATAMU BEACH

THERE WAS a jetty at the end of the garden that was surrounded by mangrove trees. Every morning we'd walk down there with coffee through a crowd of scuttling red crabs, and find monkeys performing tricks on the wooden duckboards, often with their babies. They'd sit and watch us from inside the mangrove, waiting for a rogue bit of banana.

I tried out my Swahili on a Giriami sea fisherman, who called at the jetty every morning, his boat filled with a fresh catch. He laughed at my attempts but we managed to exchange pleasantries. The mornings, filled with wildlife, 'Jambo!' and smiles, were the best part of each day.

Six months before I left Graham, we went on holiday to Kenya together. We stayed in the house of a friend from the UK – it was situated on the banks of a river estuary next to Watamu beach, called Mida Creek.

I had arranged the holiday in order to follow in the footsteps of my mother and father. I was keen to retrace their steps around Mombasa and Malindi – to see the places they'd told me about in my childhood, my dad showing me his old cinefilm on a pull-up screen.

I wished with all my heart that I had been part of my family's African story and used to pretend I had been in primary school, making up a whole host of animal friends I had made out there. I knew some basic Swahili words my parents had taught me and now practised them on the smiling staff at the house in Watamu.

The house was far grander than I'd imagined, with house workers, a chef and a manager. My mum would have loved it. Graham and I loved it too, but found it uncomfortably colonial with its security gate and guard. We found out that the staff had left their loved ones to live at the house year-round, even when no one was staying in it. And when we came back from safari in nearby Tsavo East National Park (my mum and dad had stayed at Voi) they crowded round us to see our pictures of elephants and lion. They couldn't afford the pricey tickets for the park so hadn't seen the animals.

As in San Francisco, I spent many hours in Kenya contemplating my unhappy marriage, amid a growing realisation that my husband cared nothing for me. I had to do something about it – I couldn't carry on as I was.

Despite his lack of interest in sex, my husband had shown a lot of interest in getting me into an absolutely tiny bikini for our holiday. It was made by an Australian company called Wicked Weasel and the bikini consisted of a few small triangles.

I visited a beauty salon for my first-ever bikini wax and told the beautician about my husband's keenness to see me in a tiny two-piece. She seemed disappointed that I was putting myself through the pain of a Hollywood wax just to please my husband. I had been looking at the women in his *Loaded* magazines and they didn't have a trace of hair anywhere on their bodies. Part of me still wanted to please him, so I went through with it.

It should have been an incredibly romantic and sexy holiday; all the ingredients were there. We were crashing around in a huge house, with balconies and rooftop day beds where we could lounge away the days and nights. Graham was pushing me to do a sexy photoshoot around the house and pool, in my Wicked Weasel bikini. But it was the last thing I felt like doing.

I was confused, because until now, Graham had never taken a picture of me, on holiday or otherwise, unless I'd asked him to. Two years earlier, on a beach in Bermuda, I was shocked at an image he took of me (by request) in an M&S turquoise bikini. Although I was pearlescent white, I thought I looked good and it was the first time I'd thought anything like that about my body in a long time. I was running a lot and doing Atkins. It had all paid off.

The timing of the Wicked Weasel 'shoot' didn't help. It was the day after I had recovered from a nasty bout of gastroenteritis after eating bad eggs. On the night I was struck down, we were on a sunset boat trip on Mida Creek. I felt so ill but I still have the picture Graham made me take of him holding a Tusker beer, grinning into the camera. He didn't care if I felt ill or not. The house staff cared more for me than he did over the next few days until I recovered.

The only advantage of the timing was that my stomach was completely flat and the pictures turned out to be amazing. Well, some of them did: mainly the ones where you couldn't see my face. There are a series of shots from inside the bedroom where he asked me to pose provocatively around the bed. I couldn't do it with any commitment and you can see the pain of me trying to on my face.

Even so, that Christmas, I ended up making a calendar out of the best shots for Graham and I know he took it with him when he left the marital home. Like the love letters he had kept from his girlfriend before me, I wondered if his new girlfriend saw my sexy calendar, or if she ceremonially burnt it. I also wondered what she made of our wedding pictures.

My husband only claimed one photo album when we came to dividing everything up between us – our wedding album. Not any of our amazing adventures together in Kenya, Namibia, Canada or New Zealand. Just the wedding album. I was more than happy to hand that over to him as a memory of a day when we had both stupidly bound ourselves to the wrong person. To this day, I don't know why he chose to hold on to that out of everything else. Maybe because it was a nice record of him and his family.

A year before Kenya, we'd had the two friends I'd gone to San Francisco with to stay at our house with their husbands. Elv pulled me to one side, and said that I appeared quieter, more subdued around my husband – far less confident than the woman she knew at work with her red hair and matching confidence. I didn't realise that my unhappiness was so obvious.

"You're a completely different person here," Elv said. "Where's Redwoods?"

This was the nickname she'd given me in San Francisco as we'd sat in a hot tub outside our villa in Russian River, sipping sparkling wine. We'd been encircled by towering redwood trees and she suddenly made the connection between them, the colour of my hair and the pronunciation of my name. (Try saying 'Lisa Edwards' without saying redwoods...)

Redwoods was the name of my glamazon work persona – but I'd left her at work and my friends could see what was really going on behind the facade. I was blossoming at work, and closing up again when I got home.

---

Early in 2010, I was promoted to publishing director at work and it came with a significant pay increase. More of our books were being made into movies and a TV show was starting to take off. I was thriving on the glamour and the adrenalin of it all and threw myself into my new role, spending less and less time at home.

I took the promotion as a sign that the time was right. I knew I needed to be financially stable in order to leave my husband and after years of paying for everything, I was in a weaker financial position than him. Then suddenly, here was the universe providing.

It was the day before Valentine's Day, a Saturday. I had gone shopping for a few hours in one of my usual escape jaunts from the house. I walked back from the train station and knew I was going to say it that night. I was going to tell him I didn't want to be married anymore.

I can't even remember exactly what I said, but I remember my heart pumping as I spoke the words. I remember Graham saying that if I did this to him, he'd never have me back. He cried.

When he left the house and got in the car, I knew he was dashing to get a last-minute Valentine's card and present. It was crunch point and there was no way a luxury sequinned-heart card was going to cut it now. Too little too late. I've still got that card and look at it every now and again as a reminder of the bittersweet pain of that moment – him desperately trying to cling on to me, even though it was clear I'd already got away.

A month later he looked at my disappointed face as I opened my forty-third birthday card and presents from him (an apron and a mug) and punched a hole in our bedroom door. It was the first time I'd ever seen him demonstrate anything like passion and ironically, it scared me.

I moved into the spare room while we negotiated the split and I relished the cool sheets and space to stretch out. No more snoring, no more sexual frustration, although bizarrely my husband suddenly developed a libido out of nowhere. He asked me how I was so easily able to shut off my sexual interest in him. Why was he suddenly so interested in sex with me after years of withholding it?

We were never sexually honest with each other in thirteen years, so I never really knew what he was into. There was so much we never talked about and never declared to one another. We even used baby voices when we were being intimate with each other. It's like we couldn't handle an adult relationship and the grown-up talk that came with it. We were friends, not lovers. And in time, I would realise that he bore more than a passing resemblance to my father.

As we went through the motions of separation and started packing up the house, Graham suddenly declared that his heart beat faster whenever I walked into the room. But I'd only ever seen him deliberately not look at me when I walked into a room, even if I was naked. I often wonder what would have happened if he had simply shown me the passion he felt towards me. It was all I was looking for from him ... and I'd looked for and found it elsewhere.

Even though my mind was made up on the separation, I forced myself to do the due diligence of Relate counselling sessions just to 'belt and braces' the whole decision of leaving him. I was surprised to find the female counsellor very ready to take his side (and later, my female divorce lawyer would be too – they both seemed annoyed that I was leaving my perfectly good husband and not simply putting up with everything).

The counsellor was very unwilling to see the fact that my husband spoke more lovingly about the people he worked with than he did about me. He lit up when talking about his team and referred to them as 'we'. All I'd ever wanted to be was a 'we', on the same team as him. But we were separate entities, like the oak and the cypress tree in the Kahlil Gibran poem at our wedding.

Most of our sessions consisted of Graham happily talking away with the counsellor about things that were unrelated to our marriage and me looking exasperated. I could imagine the counsellor telling her friends in the pub later that day, "I saw someone today who was throwing away a perfectly good husband for no reason at all!"

I remember coming out of one session where we both knew it was over.

"You've already made your mind up, haven't you?" Graham said.

I nodded.

We were sitting, heads bowed, on a bench in the grounds of Cliveden House in Buckinghamshire. We'd loved that place. It was sad. Extremely sad.

We both sat there, holding hands for quite some time, not saying anything. There wasn't much more to say. We were parting. The house was on the market.

Graham moved out to stay with a friend while I stayed put, but not before putting in one last house rule. "Don't bring any men into my house," he declared.

PLAY

# PATONG BEACH

## PHUKET, THAILAND – AUGUST 2010

I WATCHED the little plane on the map on the back of the seat fly its course over Europe, Asia and then South East Asia. I would be flying into Bangkok airport and then taking a linking flight to Phuket. Where I was going was somewhere 'real' travellers would probably avoid – Patong – but I needed a lovely hotel near a bustling town and that's what I got.

I revelled in everything that I take for granted now: the welcome drink of exotic fruit juice, the flowers decorating my bed and the towels sculpted into the shape of animals. It was August and the off-season, so they upgraded me to a beachfront room with a balcony overlooking the sea, framed by swaying palm trees. It was perfect. Or it would have been if I'd been on a romantic holiday for two.

One of the first things I did after I left my husband was book a holiday. I had never been anywhere outside the UK on my own but I suddenly felt the urge. I called a travel operator – how quaint! – and asked them where they could take me for a week or two for my budget. "Thailand," they said.

It was almost Bali, but crucially not Bali. I was very keen not to be an *Eat Pray Love* groupie. Thailand was where solo travellers went, knowing there would be other solo travellers. It was a well-worn path and that would give me a foundation to work from. I wanted somewhere that was far enough away that I wouldn't be tempted to fly back if I lost my nerve. A sixteen-hour flight would do it.

"I always wanted to go to Thailand," Graham said regretfully as soon as he discovered my plan. He offered to take me to the airport and I'll never forget the look on his face when he dropped me off. It said, *"Wow, she's really doing this."*

This time I didn't have to wait for him to finish three cigarettes before going through to departures, he wouldn't be making my cry at the other end for booking something he didn't like, or trying to photograph me in a microscopic bikini. This was a holiday for me and there would be no recourse to anyone else.

But oh, the despair. It kicked in on the first evening. I was in a paradise location, complete with Disney levels of butterflies dancing around the gardens between my room and the beach. I was surrounded by romantic couples and here I was on my own.

I drank cocktails at Happy Hour in a bid to cheer myself up, but I ended up crying into my Thai green curry in the restaurant. The staff didn't know what to do so they stayed away from me. I cried non-stop for three days and barely left my room. I cried for my failed marriage, the time I'd wasted with the wrong man, the time he'd wasted with the wrong woman, and the time I'd wasted with no men. I cried for what I'd done to Graham by cheating on him, because he didn't deserve it. I cried for the holiday adventures I'd had with him that I'd never have again, and I cried for the loss of coupledom. I didn't have my hand in anyone's hand and I was out there alone with no one caring.

But someone did care. Friends sent texts to see how I was getting on and I admitted that I felt miserable. I was getting up every morning to go to breakfast and wearing sunglasses because my eyes were so screwed up by all the crying. I pulled on a lovely dress to make myself feel better: a breakfast dress.

I've continued with this breakfast-dress tradition on holiday ever since. I often look more glamorous in the mornings than I do in the evenings. It's something I like to do for myself when I'm away and I recommend it. If I dress up at night, people think I'm 'on the lookout', so I dress up in the mornings instead. Breakfast dress.

One of my oldest friends from Hove days, Kay, texted with a few suggestions about what I might do to cheer myself up. There was a spa perched high up on a hill above the hotel that offered massages, manicures and pedicures and I resolved to have everything done.

I had never had beauty treatments until I'd had that Wicked Weasel wax done for Kenya. In my old life they seemed like a waste of time – who needed nice nails when you were on safari? But suddenly they were everything I needed.

With my cried-out piglet eyes I lay under towels and let a Thai woman walk all over my body. I let another woman paint my toe- and fingernails orchid pink and put matching flowers in my hair.

Afterwards, I went for a walk down to the bright white jetty that stuck out into the sea in front of the hotel. To get to it, I had to walk on a butterfly-filled path through the jungle. There were sunloungers on it with no one on them because it was the rainy season, and an ice-cream salesman downstairs. I decided to set up camp there.

I remember lying there and reading David Nicholls' novel *One Day*, in one day, marvelling that I had this glorious location all to myself. I forgot I was in crying mode and started to spend time just staring at the sea and my toenails. I found solace in a good old puzzle book I'd bought at the airport.

I texted Kay back: *"The pampering worked!"* She suggested I try a trip next – perhaps to see some elephants or a boat trip. I booked both.

I loved riding atop a naughty teenage elephant at a nearby sanctuary, where the animals were well-looked after. My animal thought it was fine to drop down into a few ditches on his way around the forest and I laughed each time he did. His mahout's conical hat bobbed in front of me as we swayed through the greenery and flitting butterflies.

I screamed with joy as the speedboat bashed against waves, hurtling towards Koh Phi Phi and James Bond Island. I got sunburned on the face and neck as I turned my head upwards towards the sun. I was coming back to life here, the wind blowing away the pain. I spent the day on and off the boat with a man my age and his young son. It was so nice to be part of a mini family for a day.

But I still hadn't gone into town on my own. I was too scared of what was outside the cocoon of the hotel. Kay looked it up for me: the town was only a tuktuk ride away.

That evening, I primed myself with Happy Hour cocktails and talked to a couple a bit older than me at the bar. I hoped that they hadn't see the piglet-eyed, wretched version of me – I wanted them to see a woman who was confident in the world in a nice dress, her nails done and flowers in her hair, all ready to hit the town. I bid them goodbye and went out to find a tuktuk.

There was a row of drivers lined up outside the hotel, all lounging in different positions around their vehicles.

"Patong?" I asked.

One nodded.

There I was, speeding towards the lights of town, a woman on her own. So adventurous! And so unnecessary: the tuktuk drive lasted less than three minutes. The town was well within walking distance and the tuktuks were there for frightened tourists like me. I laughed when I realised and so did the driver.

I hopped out of the tuktuk, heart beating fast, with the Dutch courage afforded by the two margaritas at the hotel bar. I was wearing a long purple maxi dress with a jewelled belt slung round my hips, boho-style. I looked down bustling Bangla Road filled with its souvenir shops, ping-pong bars, nightclubs and ladyboy dancers posing for photographs. It reminded me of parts of Brighton. Then I saw the bar for me – Murphy's. I knew I'd find a friendly face in an Irish pub.

I went in and pulled up a stool at the bar. There was a band on, covering Western rock songs with an impossibly beautiful Thai woman singing. In between songs, I turned to face the barman and blend into the bar. I was sure no one could see me up there, my back to the room, sipping on wine. No one approached and no one said anything, but I had found somewhere I could sit quietly and be part of the world outside the hotel.

On my second night, I knew what to do. I dressed down in shorts and a vest. I wanted to blend in more and not stand out in a long dress and a jewelled belt. I wanted to look like someone who backpacked all the time and rocked up at bars like this every day of her life, straight out of a Sheryl Crow song. There was no band on this time. Just me, facing the barman again, staying as still as I could so no one would notice me.

"Are you on your own?" an Aussie voice said.

I turned round to find a group of Aussies in their twenties bustling into the bar in brightly coloured singlets and board shorts.

"Kind of," I admitted, although I'd been doing a very good impression of being with two young women who were also sitting at the bar.

"Not any longer you're not. Come and join us!"

There were men and women in the group, all bright-eyed with their travels and good vibes. I'd seen tribes of them scooting around the island and envied their freedom. Especially the boys – it was clear that they could do anything they wanted whenever they wanted. I wanted their lives, but was that something a forty-three-year-old woman could ever have? I wasn't sure. But for now, sitting in an Irish bar with a group of Aussies for company was enough. A group of Aussies who suddenly parted in the middle to make way for their leader, Dougie.

Dougie had dark eyes and jet-black hair gelled up from his face into a Joey-from-*Friends* quiff. Dougie had the broad shoulders of a trainee Thai fighter. That's what he was doing there, he said.

After an hour of talking, he looked down at me with half-lidded eyes that showed me what he wanted. "Do you want to do a Phantom?" he asked.

"A Phantom?"

"Yeah – just get out of here without saying goodbye."

Ah my favourite – the French Exit – which I now know has a variety of different names around the world. I do it all the time – it takes away the need for lengthy goodbyes, and when people are drunk at the end of the night, they don't notice you've gone anyway.

We walked out, heads down, not saying a word to anyone. Dougie hailed a scooter taxi – the driver was a woman my age – and beckoned for me to get on behind him.

I clung on as we hurtled into the night. We stopped briefly at his hotel so he could collect a few things. The Thai woman turned to me and said, "I think he will be very good for you." She couldn't have been more right.

She dropped us at my hotel and we bumped into the couple I'd met at Happy Hour earlier. They were going to bed for an early night. I wasn't.

The next morning a pair of dark eyes and a shock of black hair peeped out from the white sheets as I made my way to the bathroom. "Where have you been all my life?" Dougie croaked, laughing.

I couldn't believe how good-looking Dougie was, and that he was in my bed. I couldn't believe that he was twenty-four. But for some reason I wanted him out of my room quickly, so that I could get my breakfast dress on and start my routine. Why I didn't keep him in my bed all day I'll never know.

I went on another boat trip and met two Aussie men closer to my age. They seemed friendly and happy to hang out with me. It was only later that I discovered that one of them had designs on me for that night – the other guy told me he'd agreed to back off and leave me to his friend. But I wasn't interested in either of them, beyond companionship in a foreign town.

We went to Murphy's Bar that evening. The guy who'd agreed to 'back off' made noises about leaving and I said I might go too. That didn't go down too well with the other guy's plan and he started to get aggressive. He clearly thought I owed him sex as he'd deigned to spend the whole day with me being a 'nice guy'. Where was his reward?

I surreptitiously texted Dougie under the table and told him I needed rescuing. He was in a bar down the road. Within minutes he appeared in Murphy's with his friends and walked over to where we were sitting. He started talking to the guy as though he'd known him for years whilst simultaneously making it clear that he wanted him gone. No sooner had he been ushered out of the pub than Dougie was back by my side.

When I returned from Phuket, I joined a website where I could be matched with younger men. I'd had a wonderful time with Dougie and I wanted to see who else was out there. Ever since I hit forty, I'd noticed younger men checking me out. Suddenly, in a way that they had never done when I was actually their age, there they were, sneaking a crafty peek.

The site I joined was Cougar Date. Again, I used my shell image as my profile picture on the website. I matched with Sam who'd put proper pictures of himself up. They revealed a tall, lean, cheekboned young man lying topless on his bed in the half light. He was eighteen.

Sam was an apprentice engineer and had his own motorbike. He would leave his parent's house early on a Sunday morning, telling them he was working overtime while they went to church. Then he would ride his bike to my house. My ex-marital house that still hadn't sold. I would lie awake in anticipation until I heard the engine switch off, the familiar click of the garden gate and the door of the kitchen quietly opening.

When I first met Sam in real life, tall, gangly and grinning, it was in my local Starbucks coffee shop. There was a guy my age in there with his young son and I saw his brain click as he realised what was going on. *THEY ARE NOT MOTHER AND SON. THEY ARE ON A DATE.* It was delicious. Sam was delicious. He was in his bike leathers and he looked delighted to see me.

The first time I took him back to my house he shook uncontrollably. He said he wasn't a virgin but I took it slowly with him. We sat for ages talking first, but I could see he was consumed with nerves and wanted to get on to the main action. I took him upstairs and he looked at me through half-lidded eyes, pretending to be in control of things while lying naked on my bed.

I was wearing the robe I always wore on those occasions, kimono-style, for easy removal. It was amazing how far I'd come in terms of body confidence. I showed him every part of my bright, white, curvy body in the harsh morning light because I was finally proud of it.

I lay next to him and kissed him softly, as he tentatively brushed his hands over my body. I could feel him quivering through his lips and fingers but as we saw each other more often, he shook less and less.

He admitted to me that he'd told his friends that he was seeing an Actually Hot 43-year-old and that's how he referred to me. I loved it and it became my new nickname. We fantasised about what would happen if I drove up to his office to see him and kissed him in full view of his colleagues. I was tempted to do it just to see their reaction.

Sam wasn't allowed to watch TV at home so after sex, we'd often sit downstairs having breakfast, watching

*Friends*, which he'd never seen. I loved those moments, almost more than the bedroom ones, curled up together on the sofa. He was the eighteen-year-old boyfriend I'd never had.

---

Every now and again Graham would 'surprise' me with a visit, intending to catch me out breaking his last house rule. He'd turn up at weekends, with a sixth sense of what I had planned, determined to patrol his territory and make sure I wasn't replacing him with anyone. But he hadn't reckoned on Preston.

In fact, I hadn't reckoned on Preston either. I met Preston after I realised that Sam was developing feelings for a girl his own age. I questioned and questioned him about it until he admitted it. Even though I knew I was simply his older-woman lover, I cared enough about Sam to know that I couldn't stomach the thought of him seeing a girl at the same time as me. I broke things off and got back on the website.

And lo, there was Preston. He was twenty-three, and again, tall and gangly, but this time blond. Whenever my ex-husband was in the house on one of his surprise patrols, I'd go out for a run or walk and meet Preston who'd be waiting in his car for me. He was the first guy I'd met who was determined to give me as much pleasure as possible and he didn't let being in a car stop him. And actually, he didn't let being in the grounds of a stately home stop him, either.

We rechristened Cliveden from the sad-bench moment of the last days of my marriage to the day when Preston bent me over among the bushes and pulled my shorts down.

The date had started in a sweetly old-fashioned way.

We'd held hands walking round the estate, sitting down for coffee and cake, just like any normal couple. I felt completely self-conscious and thought that people would be staring at us because of the obvious age gap, but they just smiled at us: another beaming couple. Maybe they wouldn't have smiled if they 'd known what we'd been doing in the bushes...

What was so unexpected about this time in my life was how comforted I felt by my frequent visits to the sexual-health clinic. I almost enjoyed it, the bravura of walking in. Here I was, finally in the land of sexually active people, going in feeling dirty and whorish and emerging absolved of all sin, and disease. It was truly like a baptism every time I visited. I always felt renewed but happy to be a sexually active member of the human race.

As time went on, I realised that us Catholics, especially women and girls, had been sold a lie about how bad sex was – there was no need to be ashamed of having it, or be ashamed of our bodies. It was all just a ruse to keep us under control. If you took the right steps, you could protect yourself from pregnancy and disease. The staff at the clinic were unjudgemental – after all, they treated sex workers and rape victims. A fortysomething woman was just another woman. One doctor I saw said there had been a rise in the number of women my age having check-ups. He asked me if I had lots of interest from younger men. It seemed I wasn't the only one in my demographic having a play around.

I WAS WEARING a red Wicked Weasel bikini and sitting in the corner of the pool, looking out over the bay. I had a view over the town– it had its fair share of tourists, but it was less 'Brighton' than Patong. It had boutique dress shops, French cafés and a picturesque broken jetty which, if Instagram hadn't only just been invented, would've been a huge selling point, especially with Thai children playing all over it.

It turned out the eight days I'd spent in Phuket in August were just a rehearsal. I'd spent three of them crying in my room and the last five had shown me what could be on the menu. As soon as I got home, I booked a second holiday, this time over Christmas for two weeks, to Koh Samui. I booked a room in a guest house with a rooftop pool by the sea in Fisherman's Village, Bo Phut, in the north of the island.

I spent my first few days shopping for new breakfast dresses and trying out the local cafés and restaurants, which all seemed to be French. I booked a few trips and went to bars alone in the evenings. Bo Phut beach itself wasn't that great for sunbathing or walking so I took taxis to Chaweng beach down the coast. It was a huge strand of golden sand filled with bars and sunloungers.

But the holiday wasn't quite the sparkling new experience I'd had in Phuket. I tried too hard to attract another Dougie and it backfired. I went on a boat trip on New Year's Eve and spent most of it with two young French men. I wore my red Wicked Weasel bikini under my shorts and lay out on the beaches we stopped at, hoping the bikini would lure them in. But they weren't interested. Another guy I'd met in a bar dropped me for a Thai woman he'd hired.

I planned to spend New Year's Eve on Bo Phut beach watching the fireworks, but it started to rain and I was alone. I felt very sorry for myself. I stayed in my room and cried.

Salvation came in the form of two Thai women. I had met them that day in the beauty salon where I went for my now-customary manicures, pedicures and massages. They were called Su and Bo – Su was my age and Bo was in her twenties.

Su-Bo shyly asked me if I would like to go out with them on New Year's Day. They would show me some places where Thai people liked to go and '*farang*' (foreigners) didn't.

What I didn't realise until 1pm the next day is that Su-Bo would turn up on one small motorbike and expect me to sit in between them. I joked that we made a '*farang*' sandwich and they laughed.

We buzzed around the island nodding and smiling to the families piled four or five high onto tiny bikes. We had a puncture and visited a Thai garage to get it fixed. Even that was fun.

Su-Bo took me for lunch at a beauty spot that had

famous penis- and vagina-shaped rock formations – Hin Ta (grandfather) and Hin Yai (grandmother) rocks. They giggled when I pointed at the white surf crashing around the base of Hin Yai. We posed for selfies together at a time before selfies. I look large and white in the pictures – the Thai women are tiny and tanned.

On the bike ride home to Bo Phut, my hair blew back as we faced the golden rays of the sunset. I couldn't help grinning. I knew I should have been wearing a helmet but I thought to myself, *if I die now, it will be ok, because I have had this moment.*

We met again later that evening to go clubbing. The New Year's Eve revellers were still going from the previous evening and we joined them at the Green Mango club in Chaweng. Su-Bo could only get in because they were with me and they stuck to me closely as the security guards checked us out. They told me that Thai women were banned from the club unless they were with '*farang*' friends. They didn't want customers being hustled for business by women who were selling themselves.

I bought buckets of cocktails for the three of us and we started dancing. I found myself up on stage with Bo after Su left us early to go back to her family. I was dancing with Andrew – a tall, dark, young Australian who was still high from the previous night. He couldn't believe I was forty-three. I couldn't believe I was either.

This was the holiday I should have had at twenty-three.

---

Before my Thai holidays in June 2010, I'd been invited by a group of literary agents to attend a conference about digital publishing. I was immediately attracted to Dean, who literally jumped over some seats to get to me. He worked in sales for a rival publishing company and we chatted flirtatiously in between introductions to various publishing luminaries.

Dean was from the northeast and ten years younger than me at thirty-three. Like Dougie, he wasn't very tall, but he had black hair, brown eyes and high cheekbones, and a body toned from lifting weights. His shoulders were the broadest I'd ever seen. I found an excuse to email him after the conference – we'd exchanged business cards – and we arranged to meet up when I got back from Phuket.

Over dinner at a restaurant near Soho, I told him my story and he confided in me that his marriage was also coming to an end. He was in the position I'd found myself in when I went to Kenya – still in the marriage but starting to plan his route out. Here, I thought, was someone I could connect with on a personal and professional level. He was funny and smart and interested in me. Yes, I'd sworn off married men, but here was one that was on the cusp of separation.

After too much wine and flirting, I flung myself at Dean at the bus stop outside the restaurant. We'd both drunk a lot and I needed to kiss him. He begged me to come back to his hotel room where he stayed on weeknights – he went home to the northeast every weekend. I said no that first time. But it wasn't long before I said yes.

We stayed in touch during my Christmas holiday in Koh Samui and met up again on my return. Things moved quickly. I'd never felt anything like it before. It was an over-whelming infatuation. I'd stay with Dean in his hotel room from Tuesday to Thursday, and go back to my unsold marital home at weekends. Our routine centred around meeting in a pub, sharing some food and wine and falling into bed in his hotel. The sex was animalistic – there is no other word for it. I made a lot of noise. I didn't even think about what the other hotel guests thought about me. I also didn't pay much heed to some of the warning signs about Dean's behaviour.

Friends in publishing reported back that he'd made cruel comments about their appearance or a joke in poor taste. I didn't really hear what they said. And then I discovered that he'd viewed our first dinner as a business opportunity – he tried to expense it on the basis that I would tell him secrets about the company I worked for and he could report back. I'd thought we were meeting as two people in publishing who were interested in each other; I didn't do networking. I decided it was just a difference of expectation and put the matter to one side.

We made plans based on a future life together. Dean's wife finally asked for a divorce in early 2011 – she didn't know about me – and we planned to have a two-centre life in the northeast and in London. It would allow him access to his two children with her who were seven (a girl) and nine (a boy).

I looked at pictures of them on Dean's phone and wondered what they would think of me, and how I would cope with being a step-parent. Sometimes he took a risk and got them to speak to 'Daddy's friend' on the phone. I looked forward to being in their lives. *Perhaps this is what I need*, I thought, *a ready-made family*.

We were openly together at publishing events and Dean joined my social group of rising stars in the industry. I noticed that he flirted with young women and gay men at these gatherings. Through me, he was getting VIP access to the publishing social scene and he worked it. I got jealous, but then told myself it was just him being sociable. After all, it wasn't as though I was a stranger to flirting myself.

Then I found myself on a romantic weekend away with him and he told me that his biggest sexual fantasy was stealing another man's wife. I know that this is a fairly popular porn fantasy, but at the time it rang alarm bells. Dean and I were sitting in a pub garden across the road from Cliveden, the location of those final moments I'd spent with my ex-husband before we parted for good. It was somewhere I'd longed to stay for a night with someone I meant something to. I didn't want to feel 'stolen'.

Cliveden was Nancy Astor's house – the first female member of parliament – and the site of many elite weekend house parties in the early twentieth century. In later years, the estate became mainly associated with the Profumo scandal – it was the site of the affair between MP John Profumo and Christine Keeler.

We'd been upgraded to the Billiard Room in the hotel. It was a 'blue moon' weekend in March 2011, my forty-fourth birthday month, and it seemed to me that all my stars were aligning. Dean was still living with his wife, but they were preparing for separation. Here I was, in my fantasy location with a man who actually desired me and wanted to share his life with me.

A few weeks beforehand, Dean had told me he loved me. At the time, I rushed to say the words back but I wasn't quite at that stage. I was still infatuated, but I was worried he'd lose interest. I knew I would love him eventually, so I said the words.

On the way back from dinner on the first night, I turned around briefly to see Dean looking at my body. It was a gaze I find difficult to describe – it wasn't pure desire, it was lascivious in a way that suggested he owned me. I baulked inside before putting my negative thoughts away.

# BODRUM BEACH

## MUGLA, TURKEY – AUGUST 2011

From my sunlounger, I looked over at Bodrum Castle, looming in the haze across the bay, its red flags flying with their white stars and crescents. I thought about the Knights Templar and ancient kingdoms. I'd arrived on the first day of Eid-ul-Fitr – the end of the Islamic fasting period, Ramadan – and the gardens of the hotel behind me were filled with tables of Turkish food and soft drinks. It was my first time in Turkey.

The Voyage Bodrum was an adults-only hotel, comprised of whitewashed buildings up the side of a hill by the Aegean Sea. It had several bars, all-inclusive, a garden and a fake beach. The 'beach' was a sandy area with shaded sunloungers where I could protect my extremely white skin. It had ladders down into the sea, where I could stand in the shallows and watch fish play around my feet while I cooled off. It was perfect for a then non-swimmer like me. I had never learned to swim, partly because of my body-image problems, partly due to being forced to jump in at the deep end of the pool at primary school.

The hotel ran a small shuttle service by boat from its

jetty to Bodrum harbour. I loved sitting behind the wizened Turkish boat captain as he went back and forth among the gulets and yachts, squinting into the sun.

Bodrum is a safe haven for a solo woman in Turkey. Like Brighton, it's a liberal town with a big gay community, and it's used to Western tourists. I found I could walk around its streets relatively hassle-free, apart from the usual, "Come and see my shop! Come and buy something!" repartee with the locals. I always made sure I covered up my knees and shoulders when I went outside the hotel, out of respect to the local culture, but there weren't many of us Westerners observing it.

I'd enter the maze of streets just behind the harbour and lose myself among the shops selling fake handbags and shoes. Those goods didn't interest me, but I liked the sound of the shopkeepers shouting to me and to each other. I liked finding a dog walking next to me on the street, purposefully, on his way to an unknown destination. I liked seeing cats basking in the shade, wearing beaded collars. I found a beachwear shop where I bought numerous bikinis and cover-ups for slinking around in back at the hotel.

The staff at Voyage Bodrum thought I was there for sex. In my very first week, a Turkish waiter whispered into my ear: "Do you want sex?" as though his approach had got results before.

"No thanks..." I replied.

He seemed surprised that I wasn't taking him up on his offer, but he shrugged the rejection off and went on his way.

I also experienced the delights of a Turkish massage at the hotel. I had no idea that this involved placing a flaccid penis into my upturned hand as I lay face-down on the massage table. I turned rigid with fear – thankfully he didn't. Eventually, I felt him gently remove his soft member from my hand when he realised I wasn't interested. I reported him to hotel management and never saw him again.

I was having my last holiday as a single woman. After our Cliveden weekend, Dean and I agreed to have our final, separate, summer holidays. After that, we would put our plan into action and be together. Dean was going to Cyprus with his wife and two children for three weeks, their last holiday as a family unit. The divorce was going ahead. I'd prepared myself for holiday celibacy in Turkey. I bought myself a ring to wear on my wedding finger to ward off potential suitors.

Dean and I called each other from that holiday – he seemed very envious of my solo status and very keen to know about any male interest I might be getting. I was getting some, from a British guy in the hotel: a Mitchell-brother type – a swaggering, bald-headed, jack-the-lad who made it clear that he wanted to come back to my room. I'd probably have let him if I'd been single and drunk, but as it was, I flashed my pseudo-wedding ring and told him that I was waiting for a guy back home to leave his wife and be mine.

"Why would he let you go on holiday on your own?!" he cried.

But no one was 'letting' me do anything. This was my last solo holiday by my own choice. The last one where I'd be that woman dining alone, with everyone assuming I was there for a sex holiday. It was also a holiday where I was determined to lose weight.

I'd been in bed with Dean a few weeks before and he'd said: "Your body was perfect when we first met." The silence that followed said it all: *"...and it's not perfect now."*

We'd been living on a diet of oily tapas and white wine

so it was hardly surprising that my body had softened from its low-carb leanness. I vowed that while we were on this break of a few weeks apart, I would lose the weight and go back to my skinnier self again. I wouldn't tell him I was doing it. I'm not sure why, but I didn't want him to know. I followed a low-carb diet for those three weeks we were apart, even in Turkey.

When I met Dean on my return, he was angry when he saw what I'd done. Strangely, he immediately started dieting himself. He'd taken up running, like me, and in fact taken up lots of the things I was into. So long as my body wasn't as good as it had been, Dean could feel better about himself, but as soon as I regained that so-called 'perfect' body, he got mad.

I knew at that point that Dean was controlling. Not in a coercive way, but in subtle ways that were an extension of what I'd experienced with my husband's house rules. He adopted my diet and exercise regime, my friendship group and even the music I liked. It was very, very strange and I'd never experienced anything like it. But once I saw the signs, I could never unsee them.

In autumn 2011, literary-festival season started and we were both due to attend one as part of our work. We decided to book a hotel room together but make it appear as though we were there separately, under our own steam. From the start, something felt wrong about it.

A few weeks before the festival, we'd been staying together at my house. We'd been invited to an eighties fancy-dress party by friends of mine and it was one of our first engagements as a fully fledged couple. Well, almost fully fledged – he was still living in his marital home at weekends. Divorce proceedings were well underway, however, and it felt like we were finally able to 'come out'. He went as Tom Cruise in *Top Gun* and I went as Adam Ant.

The friend who'd invited me commented that we 'matched' as a couple – to her it had been very obvious that my ex-husband was just my friend, not my lover. My friend was an ex-model and every time she had a party she took polaroids of people pouting and walking a makeshift 'runway'. She made us walk up and down in her kitchen in our fancy dress while she took pictures. Dean and I looked good together.

The next morning, I suddenly realised that my friend might upload pictures of the party to Facebook and tag me in them. We would be out there, together, for all our friends to see. But Dean's wife might see the pictures!

I panicked and ran upstairs to log on to my computer and check. There was a polaroid of the two of us, clearly together, posted by my friend's husband. I messaged to tell him to take the photo down and he did straight away. I breathed a sigh of relief and went back downstairs to Dean to tell him the good news. When I found him, he had a strange look on his face.

"Why did you panic so much about the photos of us going up on Facebook?" he asked.

"I didn't want your wife to see them." I wondered why he seemed so unfazed about the potential consequences.

"I thought you might be worried that other men might see them. Other men you're seeing," Dean continued.

"I'm not seeing any other men!" I responded.

Since our weekend at Cliveden, I'd slowly extracted myself from any former liaisons. I didn't yet love Dean in the way he loved me, but I could see things heading that way and it felt wrong to talk to other guys. But while he was back in his marital home I sometimes got bored and indulged in my old habit of sexting with men, especially at weekends if I'd been drinking. It was an activity that had boiled down to almost nothing by then.

I was readying myself to make a commitment to Dean and my old life of playing around was fading fast behind me. I would be a new woman, committed to one man who cared about me, who desired me and wanted the world to know he was with me. This was it, children and all. I was excited for the future.

And then the following day at work, I got a call from him. Dean had a confession to make. He'd looked at my phone while I was checking the computer for pictures of us at the party. He'd scrolled back through my Facebook messages and found a conversation from months earlier – just after Cliveden – with a former lover. I'd been bored one weekend, and resented the fact that Dean was still going home to his marital bed. Drunkenly, I'd told this guy I needed a man.

A part of me wondered why I couldn't continue to sext someone while Dean was still sharing a bed with his wife, but I could see why he was upset. I'd told Dean I'd loved him too early on in the relationship, before I actually did, because I was so worried about losing him. When I sent those texts, we weren't officially in a relationship, but we'd declared our love to one other so I'd been disloyal.

In that festival hotel room, I was being punished. Dean didn't want to spend time with me in the room – he went to the gym and worked on his newly lean body instead.

We went out in the evenings with people from the industry and he picked small fights with me in front of them. He took umbrage with something I'd said to a journalist in a pub one evening and tried to tell me what I should have said and how I should have said it. I accused him of acting like someone in PR whom we both abhorred. He got angry and we went to bed silent and tense.

I cried and cried that night in front of Dean. I repeated, "Please don't leave me!" again and again, begging for forgiveness for those texts. I was on my knees, sobbing in front of him. I think it was what he'd always wanted.

When we got back to London, the punishment continued. One night, we went for dinner as usual after work. Dean was quiet and sullen over the meal and nitpicked over what I was eating, on the carb content.

"Ok, Diet Police," I replied, irritated.

We went back to his hotel room and he sat slumped on the end of the bed.

"What's the matter?" I asked, guessing what was coming.

Dean had been talking to his wife. She was threatening to move the children to a bad school because of the divorce and he was beside himself at the thought. She was doing it to punish him for not loving her anymore, he said. She still didn't know about me.

I felt sick.

He gestured for me to sit down. "I can't do it. I can't go through with this," he said.

"Ok ... tell me," I said nervously, hoping I could turn this round.

"It's my wife and the kids. The school... I have to go back and sort this out."

"Go back and sort this out or go back for good?" I wanted to get to the point of this conversation quickly.

"I think I need to go back to my marriage for the sake of the children."

My insides dropped to the floor. Was this happening? Was this really happening?

"You can stay tonight if you like," he said, not looking me in the eye.

I stood up to leave, my legs wobbling underneath me. "I have to go," I said, hugging him for the last time.

I walked down the road towards the tube station as though I was living in someone else's life – someone who had just lost her future. I stopped in the middle of the pavement. The pain was unbearable.

I turned back and got into his bed for one last night. It was the saddest night of my life.

The next day and the next day I went to work. I stared at people and computers and pieces of paper but didn't really see them. My brain was a thick fug of anguish.

But I consoled myself with the fact that Dean was going back to his wife for the sake of his family – to make sure his children were placed in a good school and living the happiest life they could. My happiness had been sacrificed for the sake of theirs. I knew that Dean would be hurting too but he'd stopped messaging me.

It was for the best.

---

It had taken the best part of two years to sell my marital home and separate all our belongings. After Bodrum, I'd gone round the house placing Post-it notes on all the items with either my initials or Graham's on them and only a mirror was in dispute. I'd paid for it, of course, but he really liked it.

I let him take most of everything, including our car. I was the one who'd initiated the split and I was the one who was moving from the four-bedroomed house we'd upgraded to into a tiny flat in London. I didn't want him to have any reason to have an issue with me so he took most of our joint possessions. Except the mirror.

I knew that Graham had some money hidden away – 'the family millions' I used to call it – and an inheritance coming his way. I wasn't interested in it in the slightest, but I knew his family thought I was some sort of gold-digger.

It gave me the greatest satisfaction to walk away from all of it to prove a point. I was ably assisted by a lawyer who seemed to be annoyed with me for divorcing Graham, and a judge who threw out the divorce case at first, saying that it was unfairly financially weighted towards my husband. Of course it was. This was Shrapnel Man.

I got a plaintive letter from Graham via his lawyer, begging me to let him hang on to his Aunt Moira's inheritance. *Have it*, I thought. *Have it all with my blessings and know that I was never interested in your money. The fact that you and your family thought I was, tells me everything about why my decision to leave you was the right one.*

By now the surprise weekend visits had stopped and I could tell that Graham hated coming back to the house. I was spending every free moment slowly packing my stuff into boxes and arranging for most of it to be put into storage while I found somewhere to buy in London.

When the removers finally turned up in October 2011, there was a woman among them. I am ashamed to say that I was surprised. My neatly labelled boxes went into the lorry and I took one last look around.

"How are you getting to your new home?" the woman asked.

I had planned to take the train. The woman had words with her colleagues and turned to me. "Look, we're not supposed to do this, but we'll make room for you in our cabin. Please don't tell the boss."

And with that, she pulled herself up into the cabin above the driver's seat and lay on her front, grinning, over my head. She asked me what my story was and I told her the edited highlights, as we drove to the storage facility and on to my new rented flat in London.

I'd literally googled 'best place to live in London' and found Belsize Park. I didn't quite realise that this was because it was the wealthiest area, but I justified it, saying to myself that I needed a safe and lovely flat to nest in for a while. Belsize had charming coffee shops, bars and restaurants around its village 'green', complete with Banksy artwork on one of the walls. There was a doctor, dentist, gym and cinema all within walking distance and I could walk to work in fifty minutes.

I found a flat to rent very quickly – it was on the top floor of a newly renovated Victorian building and no one had lived in it since it had been refurbished. I nicknamed it the 'eyrie' because it was so high up. It had sloping roofs, views over the city and skylights filling the rooms with light. It was so clean, dry, warm and comfortable. And mine. It would be a space just for myself with no one else to consider and no house rules. I would feel safe and secure and yet free as a bird in my freshly painted eyrie, high above West London.

Dean and I started messaging each other as I was preparing for the move. He was back at home, but it was awful, he said. His wife was behaving terribly and using the children as pawns. I detected that a small door of possibility was opening again between us and invited him to meet up. He suggested that he help me move into my new place and I was delighted. I was trying to do all of it on my own. I had a sense that I might be able to lure him back into my life.

Dean cycled up to my new flat and locked his bike outside before rolling up his sleeves to help the removal people. We grinned stupidly at each other every time we passed on the stairs, arms around boxes – we would be together again. I knew it.

When we'd said goodbye to the last of the removers, Dean looked at me. "Come on, let's go shopping. I'll cook us something."

I was delighted. This was clearly his way of saying he was back in my life for good.

We bought wine to drink while I watched him cook, smiling, knowing he would be back in my bed that night.

And that was when I finally fell in love.

The sex wasn't animalistic, it was slow and it meant something different. His body laid heavily on mine, deep inside me and I felt an inner light go on as he looked at me. I finally told him I loved him. And meant it.

The next morning, I couldn't contain my happiness. The light that had switched on inside me wasn't going out. I was finally with the man I was meant to be with. Here he was, in all his glory. He took me for breakfast and we grinned at each other.

"So what's next?" I said, wondering how we were going to make our original plan happen.

"I wish I could stay with you longer," he replied, "but I'll need to go back and make sure the kids are ok."

"Oh of course. But then what? How do we do this?" I offered.

"Do what?" He looked confused. "Oh ... you thought

this all meant I was coming back? No... no... I just thought I'd help a friend out."

"A friend. You helped me move as a friend."

"Well, yeah. Isn't that what we are now?"

I felt violated. Dean had sprayed over my territory like a dog, marking it as his own. He had put his hands over everything – me, my belongings, even my food – and claimed them. Not only had he tried to usurp my social life, he had now claimed my new home. And I hated him for it.

I rolled the word round in my head. *Hate, hate, hate.*

I stomped to work thinking it. I ran round the local park thinking it. Everywhere, I thought it and repeated it in my head. *Hate.*

It's a horrible thing, to have so much hate inside you that is really love.

I threw myself into work, determined to shine brighter than ever, reclaim my social circle without him in it, and reclaim my position within the publishing industry.

I dieted, I walked, I ran. I listened to heartbreak songs on those radio stations I'd previously scoffed at, like Heart FM. I finally understood what they were all singing about. I'd never given my heart to someone and it had never been broken. Now I knew why everyone sang about it constantly. But I was veering more towards the Alanis Morissette school of rage.

Weeks passed. Dean wanted to meet up. He wanted to return the Tupperware he'd borrowed containing a portion of the meal he'd made us. I didn't want the Tupperware, but I didn't want to miss my chance to say how I felt.

I waited in a pub near his hotel, my cold glass of wine sweating condensation on to the beer mat underneath it. It was a pub we'd met in so often, as lovers, with our intimate chats, our tapas and our wine.

He came in, head bowed sheepishly. "Thanks for meeting me."

We kept it short – he didn't even order a drink.

"I just feel so sorry for you," he said, "because I can go back to my home life and family, just as it was, and pick up the pieces. You are now alone in the world. I'm sorry I did this to you."

I felt the loathing rise at the back of my throat. Was he really getting off on the idea that he'd done this to me? Getting off on raising me up on to the highest pedestal only to pull it out from underneath me and watch me fall?

*Oh no, matey boy, no you don't.*

"Yeah, but you're going back to your wife and kids. I'm free to do what I choose and you're going back to the life I walked away from. I'm sorry you have to go back to that."

I never did get that Tupperware back.

---

West London felt like home faster than I thought it would, but I struggled to afford the rent in Belsize Park. And now Dean had taken the shine off my brand-new flat in the worst way. I decided to use the money I'd saved from the sale of my marital home and buy a flat somewhere more affordable. Somewhere I had not been with Dean.

I met someone at a work dinner who told me that she'd just moved into a gold building in Kensal Rise in northwest London. They still had flats to sell and she said I really should go and view them. *A gold building!* That is what I needed after the eyrie – somewhere shiny and ostentatious, offering a dream. A new gold dream.

As soon as I stepped out of Kensal Rise Overground station in spring 2012 I knew it. This was the place for me.

This would be my new home. The gold building appeared on the horizon above the busy main road, Chamberlayne Road, and made me smile with its swagger, like it was wearing a sequinned dress in the middle of a sea of denim. I found out later that the locals loathed it, at least at the beginning, including Damon Albarn. It was a '*monstrous carbuncle*' in the faded grandeur of their Victorian streets; it was the 'B&H' building because of its matt gold finish. "Oh you live THERE," people would say when I first moved in, but as time went on, they changed their tune.

Kensal Rise was the confluence between two worlds – yummy mummies and media hipsters. This was largely down to the BBC being nearby in Shepherd's Bush but after they relocated, some of the hipsters remained. I didn't belong in either group – I was somewhere in between.

I loved the buzz of Chamberlayne Road with its pop-up pizza places and jam-jar cocktail bars. I looked at the view out of the picture window in the flat I was thinking of buying and knew I'd found home. It overlooked four railway tracks but I didn't care – it meant the nearest house was far away and no one could see me that high up. I could see Alexandra Palace to one side and the Wembley arch to the other. And if I went up onto the roof to the communal garden, I could see the City. Up there, its landmark buildings twinkled and sparkled in the night sky. I would live in the gold building and rebuild myself. I put my offer in that day and in July 2012, I put the key in the door of my beautiful, clean, white flat.

But I still heard the word 'hate' in my head on a regular basis. I couldn't let it go. Dean had taken my heart and trampled all over it. And yet ... the sound of that word softened over the course of the year. By the autumn, I could see from his social media (the parts I hadn't blocked) that his life at home was looking miserable. I felt a bit sorry for him so I emailed him: *"I'm still missing you and thinking of you. Hope all is ok."*

He wrote back that things had got really tough between him and his wife, and that he'd moved back in with his mum. He said he thought of me *'fondly'* which I thought was an odd word to use for someone he'd loved.

---

In early 2013, it was getting perilously close to London Book Fair. It was a veritable minefield where I could bump into Dean around any corner. I dreaded it.

Until I started wanting it to happen.

*"Please don't run a mile if you see me at the fair,"* I wrote in the kindest, non-hate-filled tone I could muster.

*"I won't,"* he said.

Buoyed up by hope once more, I sprang into the book fair in April, hoping to bump into Dean at every corner. It was spring and new opportunities were in the air. I'd started a new job in the adult publishing sector after twelve years in children's books. My boss had made it clear, without saying the words, that my role was going to be made redundant. A change of management was coming in with their own people and I was in the firing line. I'd got out before I was forced.

I decided to host some drinks for people in the industry on the first day of the fair at Earl's Court. Early in the evening, I discovered that one of my friends was leaving my drinks to go to Dean's drinks across the road. He was there with a handful of the friends I'd shared with him and now they were trying to see both of us.

*How strange*, I thought. I felt hurt that after our 'not

running a mile' agreement, that he'd felt the need to set up drinks at the same time as me, at a pub not a million miles away. Our mutual friends acted strangely around me, but I put it down to the weirdness of being friends with two people who'd split up.

Day two at the fair and I still hadn't bumped into Dean. But I had bumped into a mutual friend of ours, Nick, who asked me if I'd like to go for a drink with him later. He had something to tell me.

I sat down opposite him at the pub and he looked down, as though he was the one who had done something wrong. "Dean was with his new girlfriend at his drinks."

"You. Are. Fucking. Joking. Me."

"I'm afraid not. I thought you might know. You know her – it's Amanda."

"Amanda Watts?"

The Amanda I'd once tried to poach from the company Dean worked at. I liked her but noticed that she hung watchfully near us, whenever I joined him at a work event. She was married, wasn't she?

"She left her husband. She left him for Dean."

Nick said it was likely that they'd been seeing each other when we were at the literary festival. I realised that the rows we'd had there may have been set-ups to bring our relationship to an end, so he could pursue this new one.

All through those months of heartbreak, when I thought he was suffering in a loveless marriage, Dean had moved on to a younger woman and started to work through the plan we had outlined for ourselves. He had left his wife for her. They would set up home together in the northeast and London so he could see his children at weekends.

She had left her husband for him.

I'd ignored all the red flags: the stealing of my social

circle, my professional secrets and even my lifestyle. He'd even bought me a DVD of *Dexter*, begging me to watch it because the psychopathic main character was someone he identified strongly with. The number of flags placed in front of me were tantamount to a UN convention, but I had been completely infatuated and didn't see what was right in front of me. I told myself that I'd had a lucky escape, but I was devastated and once more filled with a hatred that ate away at me while he simply moved on.

In June 2013, I went back to Bodrum and this time I didn't wear any rings. I was free to do whatever I chose and I was determined that men wouldn't be on the menu. I knew that what I'd experienced was proper heartbreak and in a strange way, I was grateful to Dean for providing an intensive course on it. In one year, I'd experienced true passion and desire, fallen in love, been fucked over, and got my heart broken. People would pay for that sort of thing.

Later, I realised I'd been a vulnerable target after my marriage and that my affair with Dean had been a rebound. I wanted to believe so much that he was the reason I'd ended my marriage – that I'd found the greener grass on the other side relatively quickly, and it was all worth it in the end. But in reality, we were two people who'd bonded over a shared experience of being undervalued by our partners and discovered that the grass might be greener without *them* ... just not with each other. I'd enabled Dean to move on from his situation with an 'illicit encounter' of his own, and he gave me the crash course in love I needed to have.

As I sat among the Turkish couples on the fake beach at the Voyage Bodrum, I noticed how beautifully curvy the women were, with rounded hips and narrow waists. This was my body shape but I'd been dieting it away every chance I could, anxious to make myself as straight-bodied as possible, especially after Dean's comments. In front of my lounger, some impossibly beautiful Turkish women were eating ice-cream. Behind me there were some European women, gym-honed and scrawny, refusing the ice-cream and opting for fruit instead. I suddenly knew which side I wanted to belong to.

It was an epiphany. That moment, right there, was the one where I ended ten years of non-stop dieting. I would allow my female form to be its most natural shape. I wanted to be like the Turkish women, proud of their curves.

The hotel photographer was always stationed at the entrance to the restaurant in the evenings, taking pictures of all the couples coming into the restaurant for dinner. When I walked in, he always turned away. Dinnertime is the most difficult time of day for any solo traveller. It's a time for couples and families, for candlelight and staring into a loved one's eyes. I stared at a book or a glass of wine. More often, I was being stared at by other couples, especially the women who wondered why I was sitting alone. Every now and again someone would feel sorry for me and ask me to join their table. Sometimes I did, if they seemed interesting, but I was happier on my own, if a little self-conscious.

Finally, I'd had enough of the photographer ignoring me. On my way out one night, several glasses of wine in, I decided to confront him about it. He was so embarrassed that he took a heap of photos of me and gave them to me on a disc for free. He admitted he just hadn't known what to say to a woman on her own.

None of them did. I took the same table in the same area every day, and there was an awkward moment where the waiters decided who was going to attend to me. I got the feeling it compromised them in some way, just by being alone with them, especially the men. On previous trips I'd been assigned a woman, but this time I got Emrah.

Emrah was black-haired, dark-eyed, with pink spots on his cheeks that appeared when he was talking to me. He wrote Turkish phrases on a napkin for me to learn, practised his English and kept me topped up with wine. I told him that I'd made a decision to stop dieting.

Emrah told me about the 'kalça' (pronounced kal-cha) and how important it was to Turkish beauty standards. It was the thing that made Turkish women beautiful. The kalça was the Turkish term for the waist, hip, bum and thigh area and it was big in Turkey, in more ways than one. Here was a place that celebrated body shapes like mine. (It would still take a few years for the Kardashians to hit our screens, when kalças became a worldwide phenomenon, replacing the fashionable boy hips of the nineties. I am one of the few people who are grateful to them for validating my body shape.)

Once I got home from Bodrum I ate what I wanted. It was so liberating, to stop caring. Every single hour of every single day for at least a decade I'd worried about what I was eating and drinking. After I said yes to the Turkish ice-cream, I said yes to everything else. I ate carbohydrate like it was manna from heaven, surprised to see how much bananas and porridge added to my energy when I went out running in the morning. How had I been exercising all this time without the right fuel to power me?

I was keen to see what would happen to my body over time and checked in every day after my holiday to see if I still liked my shape in the mirror. I did.

After about six months, there were clothes that didn't fit

me anymore, but there were others that fitted better. I filled out some clothes with my blossoming top half (I've always been a classic British pear shape) and realised that some clothes only made sense when there was a curvy figure pressing out the fabric in the right places.

I packed away the clothes that were now a little tight, not knowing if I'd ever need them again, and only wore the ones that I was newly filling out. I grinned at myself in the mirror as I realised it was ok. I was putting on some weight but I still liked myself.

---

Back in Kensal Rise, I searched for new friends but quickly realised that because I wasn't at the school gates, I couldn't join their tribe. I was in the land of the yummy mummy, and I didn't fit the criteria.

I was glad that I'd had no children to tie me to Graham after the divorce, but at the same time, I hoped that his desire to become a father would now become something he could fulfil.

I knew that if I'd had a child with him, he would have left all of the work up to me, and continued his life as normal, as many men do. I would have lost my freedom and independence and be forever tethered to him and the children. I didn't want to live my life through someone else – I wanted to live it myself. "It's just what you do, isn't it?" said one friend about having children. But marriage is 'just what you do' too and I wished I hadn't done it.

I'd surprised myself by being very ready to take on Dean's children, but I knew that something had happened to me while I was with him. Something biological. A desire to have a child with him rose within me for a while, almost like a water table deep inside. It's the only time I've ever felt it. But as with Graham, my gut instinct told me that it would be a bad idea. I kept it a secret and after we split, the water table lowered once again.

I clung on to the idea that the 'right guy' would still be waiting in the wings for me. Dean had simply been the last of a string of younger men that weren't suitable candidates. And to me, he was unusual, as a young father. I'd been surrounded for most of my life by men who joked about commitment and being tied down by marriage and children. Wasn't that what they all secretly feared and avoided? They were all Chandler Bing when we talked about it in the pub. I thought I offered the perfect solution to men – a woman with no maternal urges. They could live their lives unencumbered by child-rearing, with a woman who had her own income.

And I don't think I've ever been more wrong about anything in my life.

It came as a shock after I left my marriage that I was an unattractive prospect to men my own age. In reality, there was no one waiting in the wings. All the single men that were my age were looking for someone younger – the magic thirty-five. They still wanted children, they said.

I also discovered, in my circle of partnered friends, that the men had often been the ones pushing them to have children. Some of the women confided in me that they hadn't been ready for a baby, but their husbands desperately wanted a 'mini-me' to send out into the world. In spite of mounting evidence to the contrary, those same friends told me that I was 'a catch' and that I would be 'snapped up'. But there was a distinct lack of snapping.

I wanted the same man as my husband, but a better version; someone who would be my best friend, but also desire me and love me in the way I thought I deserved. Surely there was someone out there like that. I'd thought it was Dean, but he'd been a red herring.

I started to date potential candidates like Rob, a fellow Welshman whom I'd met initially on Twitter, and then later in the local pub. On our first date, we got drunk and slept with each other. On the second date, he turned up already having had a few drinks and I raced to catch up with him. He said he didn't drink much but it was clear that he did. I did too, but by now I was a binger – nothing for a few days and then a blitz. I drew the line at turning up to a date already drunk.

Despite the inauspicious start, we continued to date and he took me to restaurants and to the cinema. It was all going well. He was a great guy in his forties – not exactly the guy I'd imagined myself with, but smart and funny. He took me to see the latest Bond film and afterwards in the bar, I ventured to tell him that I liked him.

Just that, nothing more. "I like you."

I didn't hear from him for two weeks. Apparently in this new world of dating, I'd missed the memo about not telling someone you like them. It was tantamount to saying, "I want marriage and babies."

Rob panicked and waited two weeks before sending a booty-call message in the middle of the night, hoping to recalibrate the relationship back to a more 'informal' setting. No thanks.

All the men around my age ran away from me. I'd asked one of them to go for a walk on Hampstead Heath and he'd replied with a long text message saying I was obviously looking for something serious. When had this all turned into such a minefield?

But of course, the thing these men had in common was

me. What was I doing wrong that they felt they had to run? Just before we parted, my ex-husband had said that he was looking forward to not being a disappointment to anyone anymore. Were my standards impossibly high? I didn't think so. But I was looking for something Graham couldn't offer me and maybe these new men knew on some level that they couldn't either. Plus, they could probably smell my desperation.

# DAHAB BEACH

## SINAI PENINSULA, EGYPT – DECEMBER 2013

I APPROACHED a guy in a chef's outfit feeling confident that he was Omelette Guy. There is an Omelette Guy in every single all-inclusive hotel I've ever been to. They make omelettes to order and throw in interesting local flavours. I always ask for everything. It's part of my morning ritual on holiday – watching my breakfast being made and trying to make conversation with Omelette Guy. I couldn't speak Arabic so with this one, I stuck to hand gestures.

I was yet to venture outside to the hotel garden and beach area, so after breakfast I went back to my room to coat myself in Factor 50 – another ritual – and put on my bikini with a cover-up. I packed a book, water, a towel and more Factor 50 into my bag and made my way to the beach.

Oh Dahab. You golden beauty. You captivated me that first day and you will always be beautiful to me. A huge stretch of golden sand fringed with white surf, bluer-than-blue ocean, and backed by sunburnt mountains. How could I not have known about your existence until that moment?

I placed my whiter-than-white body on a sunlounger under an umbrella and looked around at the others on the beach. There were dogs reclining in the patches of shade behind signs advertising windsurfing lessons; couples smoothing sun lotion into already sunburnt backs; waiters in crisp, white shirts carrying trays of strong coffee; a boy riding a horse through the surf, followed by a tethered camel.

That first day, I read my book and took note of the changing light as the hours ticked by. The mountains curving round the lagoon in front of me changed colour, from blue to bronze and then finally black as the sun went down behind them. I pictured Bedouin over the horizon shouting at each other in Arabic, heads swathed in fabric.

After visiting Bodrum twice, I'd looked for a new solo holiday destination. I loved being by the sea and I liked Islamic countries. My friend Kay suggested I look at Dahab, on the east coast of the Sinai peninsula, an hour north of the Egyptian tourist destination, Sharm el Sheikh. It was a windsurfing town and Kay said that I would love the place, with its laid-back, shisha vibe.

So in 2013, I decided to spend Christmas in Dahab. It ticked my boxes: it wasn't a place that everyone knew, it had surf beaches and surfers, it had mountains and mosques. Like Bodrum, I liked the sound of the word: *Dahab*. It had started life as a Bedouin fishing village and it meant 'gold' in Arabic. It was meant to be.

I confess I had rather a romantic and casually racist notion of Egypt, possibly fuelled by watching *Lawrence of Arabia* at an early age. I had the notion that an Egyptian man might carry me off into the mountains, wrapped in a Persian rug. Don't ask me where that came from, because it doesn't happen in *Lawrence of Arabia*. But from somewhere, I'd developed this idea that Egyptian men wanted to cart white women off to their Bedouin tent in the desert. I was the child of colonial parents, after all.

I was also warned about travelling to Egypt as a lone middle-aged woman. It was different from Turkey and Thailand, people said. Men would try and take advantage of me – perhaps to try and get a ticket back to the UK where they would then leave me high and dry. Everyone seemed to have a story about a friend of a friend who'd married an Egyptian they'd met on holiday, who had then run off with another woman (and her money) once they were in the UK.

I steeled myself – that would not be me. I was not going to Dahab to meet men – I was going to rest and read books. I booked the relative safety of an all-inclusive resort, as I'd done in Turkey. I'd be met at the airport and transported safely to the hotel.

I arrived at the hotel at night, having been picked up by a lone driver at the airport holding a placard with my name on it. The drive to the hotel took about an hour and I could see the outline of mountains on each side of the road as I peered out of the windows.

Once away from the airport, any light pollution slowly disappeared and the only light I saw came from the moon and stars and the car's headlights. I wondered what those mountains looked like in daylight. The driver didn't say anything – presumably because he only spoke Arabic. I had a slight fear of being alone with this silent man in a car in the middle of nowhere with no phone signal.

All the scaremongering I'd heard about Egypt had got to me. And it wasn't just about the men. I worried about terrorism – ISIS were present in northern Sinai and Dahab had witnessed three nail-bomb attacks of its own in 2006. Dahab's tourism had taken a hit as a result but had now picked up again as international visitors started to return. We stopped at various police checkpoints along the way. I later discovered that when the car was carrying a tourist it was waved through.

I was scared but thrilled to be on this adventure to a new, strange place with a beautiful name. On the way to the hotel, I spotted the twinkling lights of Dahab town further along the coast. I couldn't wait to visit it.

I was greeted by two serious men in beige shirts and trousers at reception. In Thailand I'd been shown smiles and flowers and been given a welcome drink. Here, I was barked at – I was told to sign the book and hand over my passport. I tried to smile at them to soften them a bit but it was a no-go.

I was guided to my room by another serious man in a blue uniform and found the customary towel display and flower petals on the bed. *They must have smiles deep within them*, I thought, and decided to sleep on the disappointment of my arrival.

I woke at 10am – late for breakfast – and pulled on my favourite breakfast dress, a blue and green orchid-patterned pull-on dress, strapless with a ruched bodice.

My eyes had to adjust to the sunlight flooding the breakfast room as I was greeted by the staff.

"Welcome, beauty lady," a man said.

*Here we go*, I thought.

I was surrounded by Russian tourists who shouted loudly over their food. There were beautiful, tall, skinny women tending to children, presided over by chunky, potato-headed men. This was a scene I was to witness every time I came to Dahab. How did these beautiful women end up with such awful men, who invariably started drinking vodka at 10am while their wives looked after the kids?

I did what I'd done in Turkey – I collected coffee and

orange juice and found myself a table tucked away to one side where I could blend into the background. As a solo traveller, I have to take items with me to breakfast to place on my chosen table so that other guests know it's taken. I take a book, my phone, my room keys and a wrap to throw over the chair. You'd be amazed at what people don't notice, and who I'd find sitting in my seat when I brought my food back to the table.

As a solo female traveller, I'm constantly having to maintain a balance between blending in and making my presence felt. It starts in the queue at the airport where couples or families often try to overtake me because I'm on my own. I literally have to stick my elbows out and maintain a wide stance to stop them doing it. It's as though I'm not there.

On my second day after breakfast, I was approached by a set of teeth – white and sparkling in a wide grin. I was on my guard. This was a Very Good-Looking Egyptian. I'd been warned about them. Even if he didn't want to cart me off into the desert, he would see me as his ticket to the UK. Because of course he'd want to leave this earthly paradise for a cold, grey city. Who wouldn't?

He was called Sherif. He was selling trips – boat trips, 4WD trips, trips to nearby St Catherine's monastery, and trips in a glass-bottomed boat to the coral reef. I wanted to go on all of them but booked one – the boat trip. Not being able to swim in a dive area meant that it was my only opportunity of seeing the famed fish in the Napoleon Reef.

I couldn't tell if Sherif was grinning at me because I was interested in his trips or if he was interested in me, but the glare from his smile was almost blinding. He had black curly hair that winged out to the sides. He wore a blue sports shirt and shorts, and worked the beach from a small hut to one side of the hotel. I watched Sherif go back and forth between the sunloungers in the heat. He was always grinning that grin. It was a good job everyone was wearing sunglasses.

On the fifth day of my two-week holiday, just before lunch, Sherif wandered over to my lounger. "I would like to take you out to dinner tonight," he said, grinning.

"Would you now...?" I replied warily.

"What do you think? Will you come?"

I wasn't sure. What if he wanted to have his wicked way with me in the desert?

He grinned again. "Go on... I'll pick you up at seven outside the hotel and we can go for dinner in Dahab town."

I finally agreed, flattered to have been asked by such a good-looking man, but still keeping my wits about me as to his intentions. I decided that afternoon that I still had time to opt out of going. I could always just stay in the hotel.

But I'd already glimpsed the twinkling lights of Dahab at night and I wanted so much to go there. I'd had one trip alone into the town in daylight, on the shuttle bus provided by the hotel and had been frightened out of my wits. I must have looked hilarious, swathed in my long dress and wrap, hiding my hair, my shoulders and my legs as I'd read women in public should. I found myself on Dahab main street, next to the sea, being shouted at by various shopkeepers as I looked for more breakfast dresses and battled to stay cool in the midday heat. "Cheaper than Asda!" they shouted.

There were no women anywhere to be seen. I felt self-conscious.

One shopkeeper beckoned me into his stall and offered

me tea. He could obviously see me wilting. Plus, here was an opportunity to sell me something. He sent a little boy off to fetch me a glass of tea – presumably it was his son. I sat there on a low stool, trying to cool down next to a fan. I was wearing too many clothes to do that.

The little boy returned with a small glass of brown liquid and handed it to me with a bow. I took a sip – it was hot and sweet and had a strange aroma. A few sips in and I started to feel light-headed and faint. *Oh god – what is in the tea?! What has he given me?!*

I was sitting where no one could see me at the back of his shop. He could easily bundle me into a pile of dress fabric, put me in a truck and drive me into the desert.

I jumped up with a sudden urge to get out of the shop and ran. The shopkeeper held his arms out in a 'what just happened?' gesture; the little boy put his hands to his mouth.

I ran to the place where the shuttle bus would pick me up and sat in the hot sun until it came. Breathlessly, I recounted my experience to the hotel staff and they looked at each other as I spoke – I took it as recognition of a common experience.

*The scaremongers were right! I should never have come here!*

My date that night was a few days after the tea incident, and I paced around my hotel room fleshing out my plan. In the end I decided I would only go with Sherif if he turned up alone. If there was another man in the car, I wouldn't get in. I would come back in to the safety of the hotel.

I walked out into the lit hotel car park at 7pm, and sure enough, there was Sherif, standing grinning outside a white flatbed pick-up truck, with another guy in the driver's seat.

"I'm not getting in. I'm not coming with you," I said, all covered up in my long-sleeved finery.

"Why not?! What is wrong?!" Sherif remonstrated.

"You have another guy with you."

His hands shot up in a shrug. "But we will have dinner in Dahab! You will love it! Come on..."

I stood there in the semi-darkness. What were the chances that these two grinning boys were going to drive me into the desert? Could it be that they were just taking me to the twinkling lights of Dahab for dinner?

I knew that my friends back home would tell me not to get in, but something in my heart was saying, '*Go, go!*'

*Fuck it*, I thought, *if I die doing this, then at least I will have done something exciting.*

I got into the cab of the truck and sat in between Sherif and his grinning friend. We drove towards the lights, not into the desert, as I had feared. So far, so good. The driver beeped his horn and waved at passing trucks and scooters. He dodged dogs and goats – Sherif complained loudly about Bedouin and their rogue animals. He was from Cairo and proper Egyptians didn't let that sort of thing happen, apparently.

The truck slowed and pulled up just behind the seaside buildings ... into what was obviously a taxi rank. The driver was a taxi driver, not a kidnapper.

I've laughed with Sherif so many times about that moment. He didn't think to point out that he was in a taxi because it was so obvious to him. All the drivers were his friends and they gave lifts to people to work in the flatbeds of their trucks. This one was empty because everyone was already home from work. The grinning driver was from Luxor and couldn't speak English.

It wasn't the first time I'd misread a situation like this.

Back in Kenya with my ex-husband I took to running along the road outside the house every day early in the morning, before the real heat kicked in. I passed people making fires and sweeping their shambas on the side of the road every day – they'd laugh when their family dogs ran out to 'greet' me. It must have been funny seeing a lumbering white person in the land of professional runners.

I always got to a certain point and turned back. I was afraid of a group of men on motorbikes sheltering under a big tree. They would stare with serious faces at me whenever I got near and I'd already been hissed at by beach boys touting for business.

Eventually I told one of the guys in the house where I was staying that I was scared of running past this group of men.

"They're taxi drivers," he said, matter-of-factly. "They're just wondering if you would like a ride home."

Much, much later I would realise that my poisoned-tea moment in the Dahab shop was a panic attack. I had misread my own panic as a powerful sedative and it was no wonder that the Egyptian shopkeeper and his son had looked so shocked at my reaction.

Sherif took me through the winding streets to a restaurant called the Crazy Mummy. We sat among cushions on the floor, surrounded by candlelight and spray water bottles for use against the ubiquitous cats. Fairy lights were strung around the curving trunks of palm trees.

It was here that I first met Bufra, the matriarch dog of Dahab, named after a make of roll-up paper (like Rizla). She's the only dog I've ever met with an actual smile on her face. It appeared to be because she had a scar on the side of her jaw pulling her face into it, but she duly smiled into the camera for me and then lay comfortably next to us on her side while I chatted with Sherif.

The grin was in full force. He spoke in Arabic to the guy serving tables in the restaurant, occasionally checking with me that I liked things like 'Baba ganou' – he didn't pronounce the 'sh'.

He told me that he lived and worked in Dahab but his family were back in Cairo – his parents, and a sister with a husband and baby. He had many friends in Dahab, made over the years of working on the beach and in different restaurants. He talked about how it used to be before the 2006 bombings, and how he had been in Aladdin restaurant near the bridge when one had gone off (he pronounced it *Al-adeen*). He said that people had run into the sea to escape the nail bomb, and he'd seen things he didn't want to describe. He said help came very late, and so did the official government visit, when suddenly the emergency services were everywhere.

Twenty-three people had died in the bombings and eighty were injured – mainly international tourists. The town had taken a huge tourism hit and again in 2011 after the revolution, and there were only four other people in the Crazy Mummy apart from us. But, he said, people were coming back to Dahab, crucially the Germans.

"The Germans are coming back," was a phrase I would hear repeatedly from Sherif and his friends. They were always hopeful about the future, never downhearted. "What can you do?" I'd hear them say. "All will be good, *inshallah*."

After an hour or so, a tall, equally good-looking Egyptian man joined us – this was Ahmed, a friend of Sherif's. Had he come to vet me, to make sure I was good enough for his friend? It seemed to be the case.

Ahmed had a British-Egyptian girlfriend and his English was as good as Sherif's. They sat and smoked cigarettes together and ordered beers. Ahmed was wearing a beanie hat and Sherif a padded jacket – they both agreed that it was cold and I would need warmer clothes than my denim jacket. It was December and 21 degrees celsius at night.

Ahmed asked me questions about my trip to Dahab. I told him the taxi story and we all laughed. I think I'd passed the test.

After the meal, Sherif escorted me back to the taxi rank and the same driver grinned at me. I'm not sure he even realised the mistake I'd made.

Back at the hotel, I removed the comedy towel creations from my bed and slid in. I'd done it. I'd had an adventure and survived. I'd been out with a Very Good-Looking Egyptian and I had not been kidnapped.

I had discovered some more about Sherif's life there, away from his family, and realised that he was reliant on friends like Ahmed – a framily – just as I was in London.

The next day on the beach, I was approached by the grin again. "You had a good time last night?" he asked.

"Yes, yes I did," I said.

"We will do it again. Tonight?"

"You're keen!" I laughed but I was secretly delighted that he was still interested in seeing me. Sherif was twenty-six and I was forty-seven.

Later that evening, we drove into town again, this time to 'Friends' restaurant. We walked through the cushion-strewn ground floor, which was a wooden deck jutting out over the sea, the water sloshing around underneath us. I could see fish moving around in the lit waters. We climbed the wooden stairs up to the roof and found a neon sign saying: '*Come here a stranger, leave a friend*' and cushions to sit on, next to stained-glass lamps. The moon and stars shone overhead; the waves glinted with silver light. It was incredibly romantic and Sherif knew it.

His friend Mo introduced himself, another one of the framily. He had his long curly black hair pulled back in a ponytail and wore jeans and a T-shirt with Bob Marley on it. He worked at Friends. Arabic was spoken, smokes were had, small packets were exchanged. I had no idea what was going on, but I liked being with Sherif, so I snuggled up to him on the cushions and looked at the night sky. He told me that he couldn't believe it when he'd seen me on the beach. He said he thought I was an angel, I was so bright white. He later changed that description to 'great white shark' and called me his 'beautiful shark' from then on.

He loved my white skin and my shape – my paleness and my *kalça* seemed to be popular in Turkey and Egypt in a way they never were in the UK. Sherif was 'black', as he put it – his skin darkened by working on the beach and windsurfing. I didn't even know Egyptian surfers existed until that first holiday. They grew their hair long and curly and wore board shorts. They squinted out over the ocean and rode the wind and waves with their friends. Who knew? It was so unexpected and delightful.

I was entirely happy for Sherif to kiss me on the roof of Friends. My Egyptian surf boy with a smile like starlight.

The next day, I met the rest of the framily on the beach at Dahab lagoon. Sherif walked me over to a small white hut where I'd already seen a huddle of surf boys staring out at the ocean, in between maintaining windsurf equipment and shouting at each other in Arabic. One of them, Amir, held his hand out to me. "Welcome," he said, motioning for me to go inside.

Sherif left for work so Amir and the boys made space for me in the hut on a sheet of flower-patterned lino. We all sat cross-legged around it, Amir serving tea. "This is Sherif's friend," he announced to the group. "We must call her 'sister'."

I was really touched by Amir's attentiveness and care. I was worried that I was wearing enough clothes – nothing on my shoulders – but at least my bikini was covered by a strapless breakfast dress.

Amir had the best English so he chatted with me over tea while the others sat quietly. He had a little boy of four who didn't like the water and he was teaching him to swim.

"I can't swim either!" I said.

Amir was shocked. Why would anyone come to Dahab if they couldn't swim? It's a world-renowned dive centre. But I loved being around people who were surfing and diving.

There was something in the vibe of these places that I loved. The optimism of a neverending horizon, the fresh sunlight every morning, the dogs that believed they owned the town (they invariably did) and the humans that congregated there, unrelated but forming support groups of their own.

I was slowly being introduced into Sherif's group and I was delighted to find a band of young men who looked out for each other, who looked out for me, and called each other 'habibi' (meaning 'beloved') and 'prince'.

After a few nights at Friends and some serious snogging under the stars, I agreed with Sherif to go to a place where we could sleep together. He made a few calls in Arabic, and we walked to a Bedouin area of Dahab where he was handed a key by a man who stared at me. I felt too ashamed to look back at him. Here I was, the classic white-woman tourist sleeping with a Very Good-Looking Egyptian.

Sherif led me into a room with a sofa with no legs and rugs everywhere. The bed was a mattress on the floor in the other room. The bare-bulb lighting gave the whole thing an air of sleaze. I felt the rising panic I'd felt in that shop not so long ago.

I was not this woman. I couldn't do it.

I realised Sherif had locked the door. What if he kept me in there and refused to let me leave?

"I want to go," I said quietly.

"What?! Come on..." he said in surprise. "What's wrong? Why do you want to go? Everything is ok..."

But everything wasn't ok. I felt like a whore, there in that harsh light and basic room with everything on the floor. Later I would realise that rooms like this are standard in Dahab but to my fear-filled eyes it all looked dirty and uncared for. We'd paid the man and I was worried Sherif would make a fuss, but he just shrugged.

"Ok, let's go," he said quietly. "It's ok."

I have never felt so relieved to leave a place in my life and to see what sort of towel animal awaited me on my bed that night.

I was amazed that Sherif took it so well. Perhaps he'd found himself in this position before and knew that Western women freaked out when they saw Dahabeyan rooms for the first time. I don't know. I didn't ask. I did ask why he didn't take me to his own room. He said it was because his roommate was there with his wife and she wouldn't approve, but I wasn't sure. Part of me wondered if it was his wife that he was hiding there. (It wasn't.) I was suspicious of everything.

A work friend had given me the name of a British friend

living in Dahab – Ali – and I contacted her from my hotel. I took a short taxi ride to her home – she was a young Bohemian artist, renting out rooms in her small villa to earn money. She gave me tea and we sat on her floor cushions beside her big white dog.

There was a Bedouin family living next door to her – she said they had a new baby and would I like to go round and visit? I was delighted. She told me that the baby had been longed for. It was a love marriage with an age-gap – a rarity among Bedouin it seemed – and now they had the gift they had been waiting for.

Next door, Ali spoke in Arabic to an older woman in a burqa. The woman smiled and reached out for my hand. "Welcome," she said.

We were shown through to a room at the back of the house and it was like a nativity scene inside. There sat young Laila, also in a burqa, holding little Aida. They were surrounded by all the women in the family. The baby was beautiful with her shock of black hair and I told Ali to tell Layla. Layla gave her thanks in English, beaming with pride.

I was given a glass of helva, a tea made from fenugreek, that I was told by Layla was "good for women". I wasn't told in what way it was good for us, but drank it anyway.

We all sat there beaming at each other, Ali speaking in Arabic with the women from time to time. "They are inviting us to the goat sacrifice tonight," she said. They'd waited seven days after the birth to celebrate their new baby and today was the seventh day. "But I'm vegetarian so I don't want to go," she added.

I hid my disappointment. I went back to the hotel and told the guys there and they said, "Oh! You should go!! It is a very special time!!" But going on my own to a Bedouin goat sacrifice was a stretch too far.

On the day I left that first holiday in Dahab, I went to say goodbye to Sherif in his little hut on the beach. He called me his great white shark again and I laughed ... and cried.

"Don't cry," he said, as he made me some tea. "It will make me sad."

But I had left a little piece of my heart in that place, next to the Gulf of Aqaba in a town full of Egyptians, Bedouins and their animal community. I knew I would have to return, not only to see Sherif, but to revisit everything else without the fear and trepidation that I'd had the first time round.

I'd even been scared of the dark there, and when Sherif walked with me along empty moonlit streets I'd been afraid to go very far in case... in case... I couldn't say exactly what might happen, when he asked me. I realised later that Dahab came alive after dark when it was cool enough to actually do things. Darkness was daylight to Sherif and his friends.

I booked a return visit as soon as I got back to London. I Facetimed Sherif with a terrible connection caused by the strong Dahabeyan winds. It made his voice go robotic and his face freeze in different stages of The Grin.

---

Four months later – in April 2014 – I was back in Dahab. I'd booked an Air BnB in the town so that I could see Sherif more easily. It was in Asalah – the Bedouin part of Dahab, which I'd barely visited last time. Sherif seemed keen to keep me at the Mashraba end – where the tourists were –

even though my guidebook said Asalah was more interesting, where all the divers congregated. He didn't seem to know the place when I described the street it was on, but he was keen to know who owned it. I guessed that he knew too many people at that end of town and was hoping I'd switch to a property he was suggesting in Mashraba. But I wanted to be in control of this situation. I wanted to choose the place I would stay and know who owned it – she was a British woman called Mandy.

I decided to be candid with Mandy in our email exchange and say that I was hoping my Egyptian male 'friend' could stay. She gently reminded me of what I already knew – that what we were doing was illegal – he wasn't allowed to stay overnight with a woman of any creed if he wasn't married to her and we could both get in trouble for it. She said that hotels and Egyptian-owned properties were a no-go, but foreign owners like her turned a blind eye. She was married to an Egyptian herself and familiar with the predicament. She said that the Egyptian police disliked seeing young Egyptian men happy with Western women and made a deliberate effort to make sure they stayed away from each other. She warned me to be careful when entering the gate of the property and to keep an eye on who was watching us.

I was glad I'd told her, and I was glad she was equally candid. It was obviously a fairly common scenario and it did explain some of Sherif's trepidation about this new arrangement. He needed to be in control of it because he knew we could be dragged away by the police.

I was met at the airport by Mandy's recommended taxi driver and arrived at the apartment at lunchtime. It was perfect, with large airy rooms and Islamic decorative features. Unlike the room I'd visited with Sherif, it was freshly plastered and had clean sheets on the bed (which had legs), jewel-coloured cushions and tasteful ceramics. I had the ground floor with a wet-room-style shower, a large double bedroom, and a kitchen leading out into a small garden. There was a hammock to swing in and I found a tiny tortoise in one of the raised beds of succulent plants.

As I looked around the garden, I spotted the minaret above my head. The apartment was right next to a mosque. I loved the sound of the muezzin around the town – there were about fifteen mosques in total. When the call to prayer sounded at various times of the day, it sounded like a choir of voices coming from the sea. It made me think of the sound of morning church bells in Venice.

Sherif arrived on my doorstep after work that evening and although he was pleased to see me, the first thing he did was case the joint. He complained that I'd booked somewhere right opposite a mosque. People would see him coming in! The noise would wake us up! Although Sherif wasn't an observant Muslim, for him it was like being next to a church where he knew the priest and the congregation. He'd have to walk past them every day to visit a scarlet woman. And that wasn't all. Sherif complained that there were Bedouin families all around with their children and goats on the street at night. "They are always watching!" he complained. I reminded him that all of Egypt was always watching, based on the evidence so far. It was practically a national sport.

It was curious to hear him voice these problems with the nomadic Bedouin who only came to Dahab during the winter, after spending summer in the mountains. They owned all the land there and Egyptians from other parts of the country seemed to resent them for it. It reminded me of the issues that people have in the UK with the traveller community. If you are not rooted to one permanent place, people are suspicious of you.

Sherif's initial jitteriness settled down into a resignation that this was where I would be staying and this was where he'd have to come if he wanted to see me. I don't think he liked me being in control of the situation and it made him act strangely.

During my stay he would spend nights with me and days at work, but in between go on secretive missions to who knows where. He'd come back late – high after smoking weed or drinking beer – a little like he needed to assert his independence. He wanted me to be waiting for him in this house but I got sick of waiting and went to Friends restaurant on my own. No doubt his Mo told him I was there and he would turn up eventually. I wasn't going to wait around in a house for any man.

After about three days of this behaviour, I had it out with him. He immediately apologised for acting 'crazy' but didn't say why he had been. I reminded him that I'd come all this way and rented this place just so we could be together and this was not what I'd pictured. I'd already escaped from men who treated me badly and I didn't need another one. He realised I was serious and softened.

We were woken the next day, as we were early every morning, by the sound of the muezzin. "I told you," he said, but then kissed me awake and stroked my body.

Sherif was a really passionate lover and seemed to take pride in his ability to please a woman. He told me that the boys regularly discussed how many times they'd managed to have sex with a woman in one night and attributed the number to how beautiful she was, rather than their own prowess. I think we'd managed five times in one night so he was especially proud. But there was a point where I started to wonder if Sherif was taking something to improve his stamina. Our nights had turned into Olympic-level sex marathons, with him going and going and going until I had to beg him for a rest.

I had noticed that Viagra was freely available in pharmacies in Dahab – "for the Russians," one pharmacist told me. He was sitting behind a huge display of Viagra boxes, tending to my mosquito bites that first time in Dahab. (I'd made the classic mistake of dining outside without covering up or wearing spray on my first night and been eaten alive.)

I asked Sherif if he was taking Viagra.

"No, no!" he remonstrated.

But I was sure he was. Mainly because I could tell when he hadn't taken it and normal service was resumed. Those are the nights I got some sleep.

I became increasingly concerned that Sherif was living a secret life away from me. There was something always hidden with him – he wasn't open and honest by nature. It was like he'd been trained not to tell me the full story of anything, to hold something back, even if what lay behind the surface was completely benign.

―――――――

I was in Dahab during the May 2015 UK general election and protested to Sherif about something going wrong with my proxy vote. A friend was trying to sort it out for me.

He told me he remembered the Revolution, the Arab Spring – three days in Dahab when he and his friends were free to talk about anything in public. Three whole days before the government cracked down again and they were unable to share information without fear of arrest. I was suddenly aware of my privilege.

"Poor me!" I exclaimed as a joke. "Poor me and my inability to cast a vote in a democratic election while on holiday in Egypt!"

"Poor you!" he replied, laughing.

It became a standing joke between us. Sherif was unable to even leave Dahab on a bus without the police asking for his papers. No wonder he held back on information. What would people do with it if they knew everything that he was doing?

"Poor you!" he'd grin when something 'bad' happened to me, like my phone being covered in mango juice. The gold phone I could immediately replace at home from my golden flat.

One day we went to a beach far away from the tourist area with Ahmed and his wife, Mariam. After the taxi dropped us off, Ahmed and Mariam wandered to the water's edge and I sat with Sherif on a log as he took out a small bag of weed and proceeded to roll up.

I decided to take a dip while he was smoking. I must have been in the sea for only a few minutes when I heard the familiar shouting in Arabic. I turned round and Sherif was on his feet, remonstrating with two policemen.

I walked up to them to see what was going on. Sherif had not noticed the police car creeping up on him as he rolled up. He had attempted to hide the bag under the log but they had seen him do it. They found it immediately and bundled him into the back of their van.

Ahmed and Mariam stayed in the sea. *Some friends!* I thought.

The two policemen turned to face me and my stomach attempted to vacate my body. I tried not to show it. "Is he your friend?!" they barked.

"Yes, he is," I stated confidently, staring back at them.

They didn't respond. They turned back to the truck, with Sherif sitting in the back, peeking out plaintively, and drove him away.

Ahmed and Mariam returned, telling me not to worry – they knew what to do. As Ahmed quickly made a series of phone calls, Mariam told me that if they'd stayed with us, Ahmed would have been arrested too. Far better for them to keep their distance and then follow what seemed to be a prescribed plan as soon as Sherif was taken away.

Ahmed called the dealer and told him to switch his phone off and leave home right away for a few days. The police would force Sherif to give them his number and they would turn up, he said. They would take the bag of weed for themselves and also help themselves to the dealer's stash. It was well-known and unsurprising that the police didn't report these incidents back to head office – they just took the weed for themselves.

After the calls had been made, we sat round wondering if we should go to the police station – perhaps I should go, because the police wouldn't arrest me.

"They don't touch tourists," Ahmed said.

I started to see the movie of this moment play out – me remonstrating with the guards and thrown in an Egyptian jail against my will, dirt smeared across my face. Someone would have to come from the UK to try and get me released. We would fight together to get Sherif released...

But just as I was getting carried away, Sherif appeared, walking along the road like nothing had happened. The police had got the number of the dealer from his phone and taken his weed. That was it. They were probably already on their way to the dealer's house and they wouldn't find him there. This was a well-practiced, cat-and-mouse routine. Sherif was angry, but mainly at losing his weed.

More seriously, here was another reminder of the privileged life of freedom I was living. I could fly here and there, to Thailand, Turkey and to Egypt, and Sherif couldn't. He would be asked for his papers or raided by police every week of his life and he took that as normal. Here, I could smoke weed on the beach and get away with it but he couldn't.

I wondered if these restrictions were partly responsible for Sherif never taking me, as he'd promised, time and time again, to various parts of Sinai that he knew and loved. He told me about Blue Lagoon, "only an hour by camel" from Dahab, where we could camp under the stars, but we never got there.

# RAS ABU GALUM BEACH

## SINAI PENINSULA, EGYPT – OCTOBER 2015

WE CLIMBED aboard the small blue and white boat crewed by two silent Bedouin men, who were cowed by the chatter and windswept confidence of a group of women. Our bodies were all respectfully covered, but we had our swimwear on underneath the swathes of fabric.

The men helped us off the boat at Ras Abu Galum, and our arrival was awaited by a Bedouin woman and her small daughter, who would be preparing lunch for us. There were six of us – me, Mona, an Egyptian hotel manager; Melissa, an artist from Switzerland; Zahra, a married Egyptian woman; Suzanne, a German woman who'd married a local and ran a seafront restaurant, and Anita – a London numerologist who now lived near St Catherine's Monastery with her Middle-Eastern husband.

We sheltered from the hot sun under a wooden frame covered in fabric and got down to our swimwear. There were rocks and plants in the water and I kept to the shallows with Zahra, who couldn't swim either. The rest of my new friends swam far out from the water's edge and I so envied them. But still, I was there and that was enough.

I was at the end of a terribly stressful two years in a very toxic publishing environment. I'd survived it but I needed my spiritual home in Egypt. I'd been locked in combat with a colleague who didn't like me "pointing out his inconsistencies". He was a brilliant gaslighter, swearing one day that a book was black, and next, lashing out at us because he'd said it was white all along. He loathed editorial people like me because we noted everything he said and reminded him of it – I ended up carrying around a dossier of everything he'd said in meetings in detailed minute form. He hated it.

I internalised the stress and began to have heart problems – huge, great, thumping palpitations that frightened me. I was dealing with a bully who would stop at nothing until he 'won'.

I started to walk to and from work along the Grand Union canal. The journey was almost eight miles in total but it was the best part of every day. It was the only thing that kept the stress from destroying me emotionally and physically. With every step along that towpath, I worked through the trauma of the day. I realised how much there was to see: people making coffee in the mornings on the roofs of gaily painted barges; cygnets bobbing in a row behind a pair of swans; bright-green duckweed covering the surface of the canal in summer; the sound of carnival steel bands practising in the early summer evenings. The gaslighter had actually done me a huge favour.

When I finally left that job behind in March 2015, I immediately booked flights to Dahab. Mandy's villa was already booked up, so this time I agreed that Sherif could book us a place to stay in Mashraba. He'd put up with my Asalah apartment but the location made him too self-conscious. As he was so well-connected, I knew he'd find us something lovely and not too expensive.

I dreamt of mornings waking up near the sea, having coffee looking over the roofs of Dahab. I thought Sherif might be waiting for me after my flight, with fresh flowers in the kitchen, a fresh salad chopped, waiting to take me in his arms and kiss me.

The reality was rather different. Like the rooms he'd taken me to when we first met, this was a four-roomed ground-floor apartment with no view of anything – just tiny windows covered in broken metal bars. Everything seemed to be yellow and dingy – the kitchen work tops, the floors, the bedspread, the walls, the curtains. It reminded me a tiny bit of my mother's house where cigarette smoke had stained the walls. It was like a prison.

Sherif said he had been promised the top floor, but the landlord had given it to a member of his family who was on holiday. I smelled a rat. Not literally, but I knew Sherif had just left it to the last minute to find somewhere for us.

I managed to stay for one night and lay awake for most of it. Sherif was happy in the dinginess. I was not.

The next day, Sherif went off to work and left me alone. He said that there was a hotel next door where I could get breakfast, so I pulled on a breakfast dress and went through the gap in the hedge in between the two properties to see what it was like.

I found an oasis. The Sheikh Ali hotel was all space and air, water and tiling, and cool cleanliness. I ordered my regulation omelette breakfast and read my book with a cat curled at my feet.

Mona, the manager, fresh from her morning prayer, greeted me and asked me what I was doing in Dahab. I was surprised and glad to see a woman in such a senior position in a hotel, with her dark hair wrapped in a scarf, wearing a Zara long-sleeved top and trousers.

I asked her about the hotel prices and she showed me a room. It had a cupola in the ceiling with a light in it, acres of shiny tiled flooring and a spotless bathroom with lights over the wide mirror. I could pad about in there and feel free. I booked it for the rest of my visit. Sherif's contact could keep the money I'd paid up front for the yellow room.

I waited for Sherif to return to the apartment with my bags all packed. "I'm going to move next door," I said.

He looked shocked. "Nooo!! Why you move there? The lady who manages it is bad. She tells her husband what to do and he is a nice man."

Unfortunately, this made me want to stay in Mona's palace even more. It became evident as time went on that Mona expected equality in her marriage and her husband gave her that. Because of this, and because of her senior job, Sherif and his friends were dismissive of her. To me it sounded like she wasn't afraid to call men out on their bull-shit and that made me like her even more.

Finally, the hotel was owned by a Bedouin family. I knew how Sherif felt about that already. But I was happy. Sherif decided to stay in the yellow apartment and I, to my shame, visited him there at night after we'd been to dinner. But I always returned to my beautiful hotel room, happy and relieved to slip in between my cool sheets, to shower in the spotless bathroom and go to bed on my own.

I placed all my things – books, dresses, toiletries, laptop – around the room and spread out on the bed. How could I have believed that Sherif could provide something like this? It was a product of the romantic fantasies I'd had in my head – in reality, Sherif was poor and I was relatively rich. I felt ashamed of my privileged expectations.

In the mornings, Mona and I would chat about clothes, places we had visited and books we had read. One day, she invited me to join her and a group of female friends on a boat trip to a nearby beach called Ras Abu Galum. I loved the sound of the words. We would have lunch there, she said, and she knew I would like her friends. They were from all over the world.

I was absolutely delighted and couldn't wait to tell Sherif in the evening when we went for dinner. He was immediately suspicious. Of course he was. A group of women he didn't know, one of whom he didn't like because she was outspoken, was inviting me out on an adventure. *Tough luck, dude*, I thought. *Women round here make their own entertainment.*

Two days later, I was packed and ready for a boat trip and a day on the beach.

Anita the numerologist joined me at the water's edge and spoke about her life in London, and then in the Sinai desert. She had long silver hair and a wisdom I craved. She spoke about the universe directing her down a certain path and that numbers showed her the way. I said I had been pulled to Dahab again and again, and she interpreted it as the universe directing me there. She said that she had found happiness in Sinai with her husband. They had a small farm and she ran numerology retreats from there. She had dogs. I was tempted to go there. She said I would be welcome at any time.

I spent most of the day hanging on Anita's every word. This woman was the most natural I'd ever seen – unencumbered by the pressures of trying to look younger than her fifty-three years. She was as she was and I was envious. I'd had years of trying to maintain a version of myself with dieting, hair dye and makeup, but Anita seemed so rooted in her own skin; so clear-eyed and happy.

The young daughter of our cook for the day looked at us

shyly behind her flowing black hair. I'd seen young girls like her – maybe nine or ten years of age – wandering around Dahab, selling jewellery or fruit. I'd questioned their safety and Sherif had reassured me that they were quite safe. He often stopped to speak to them and gave them money. It seemed to be something that everyone did.

I found out that the reason these young girls were free to roam was because they were not yet sexually mature.

"This mother is trying to make her daughter look young for as long as possible," Mona explained. "When she gets her period, she will be housebound until she is married, along with the other adult women in the family. Her mother will want the girl to remain free for as long as possible. When her period starts, she will hide it from the men in the house for as long as she can."

I had escaped from a community of men – albeit a lovely supportive one in Dahab – and found an oasis of women at Ras Abu Galum. Only Zahra seemed concerned about her husband's reaction to this non-traditional group outing and didn't even get as far as removing her outer layer of clothing.

We ate a dish of spiced chicken and rice and lay in the shade to digest it. The conversation inevitably turned to men, and quietly, I admitted that I was seeing an Egyptian. The women had already guessed, of course.

I asked Suzanne about the feasibility of a life out there married to an Egyptian man. She said she had found a good one, and enjoyed a true partnership with him. But she and the others warned me – Egyptian men were not always good and some of their non-Egyptian girlfriends had run into problems when they'd given up their lives to move there. You had to be sure about what you were doing and the man you were binding yourself to.

The thought had entered my mind – to live in this place that made me so happy with Sherif. But deep down I mistrusted him and his secretive ways, and after several visits I realised that I had fallen in love with the place and its people, not the man.

On the way back to Dahab from Ras Abu Galum, the sun was setting behind the Sinai mountains. I sat behind the swaddled, sinewy Bedouin who was crouching at the stern, manning the tiller of the boat.

I remembered that first Thai speedboat trip and the feeling of the sun on my face and the wind in my hair. Here I was again, this time in the company of women from around the world: Muslim, Christian, New Age and Atheist. I'd lost my Catholic faith decades earlier.

That night I chattered on and on about the day. Sherif was keen to know if a man had been with us. He seemed unable to believe that a group of women could act so freely without a man to supervise them. Yes, there'd just been the two boat crew, I said.

"No husbands?" he asked.

No husbands. No men monitoring or controlling proceedings – just some wild women by the sea, hair flowing free. No one watching apart from a shy young girl behind her mother's skirts.

I knew on that trip that things were coming to an end between me and Sherif. Something had shifted, mainly that I was discovering Dahab for myself. I had found a cool airy home in the hotel and been adopted into Mona's matriarchy. These women were strong and independent and they were showing me how life in Dahab could be. I could, if I wanted, choose to marry Sherif, but something was telling me that he would, once married, impose restrictions on my life and want to keep me in a yellow house. I was worth more than that, even if it meant being on my own.

I returned to Dahab one more time after that and flew out again four days before the Russian Metrojet bombing at Sharm el Sheikh airport in 2015, killing 224 tourists and stopping all flights from the UK for a few years. I somehow knew it was my last visit and auspiciously wrote a blog post – an ode to this special place – called 'Goodbye to Dahab'.

On that last trip, I had been bothered by a male stalker – a British man called Cliff who'd found my blog posts and got in touch. He'd assumed that I'd need a male companion while I was in Dahab and sent me a torrent of direct messages on Facebook, Twitter and on my blog. I was very scared, and it was the first time a man had scared me in Dahab. (It's always British men that hassle me on holidays – never the locals.)

Then he upped his game, delivering a hand-decorated letter in person to the hotel, suggesting I join him on a spiritual journey in the mountains of Sinai. I told the male staff behind the desk.

"Don't worry, we know where he is staying. We will sort it out."

To this day I don't know what they did but he stopped contacting me. No one messed with the Bedouin it seemed.

On the first day of my final trip, I told Sherif that I wouldn't be sleeping with him anymore. He didn't believe me and kept trying to kiss me, but my mind was made up. I saw him a few times for dinner, but I always refused to go back to his apartment afterwards. I had found my oasis in the hotel and I didn't want any more dingy rooms or Viagra.

I couldn't shake the idea that Sherif wanted a better life via a woman – whether that was here or back in London –

where his friend Ahmed had now moved with Mariam. And who could blame him if he did?

He said that I would always be special to him and be in his heart, even if we weren't together, but in reality that lasted only a few months after I returned to the UK. He made a last-ditch marriage proposal the following Christmas but when I said no, he blocked me on every online platform.

I had made the right decision.

---

Post-divorce, I took pride in flying solo, literally to places like Thailand, Bodrum and Dahab, but also to bars, restaurants, clubs and even gigs in the UK. I became frustrated by always having to wait for friends or colleagues to be available before I could go for a drink or a meal out, so I often took myself.

The first time I went to a bar alone in the UK, I chose a nice busy pub in Kings Cross. I took a newspaper. I sat on a stool at the bar, as I'd done that first time in Thailand, and ordered a large glass of white wine. I read every inch of that newspaper and even did the crossword, glancing up every now and again as the post-work crowd ebbed and flowed around me. No one stared, no one said anything, not even as much as an 'excuse me' to elbow closer to the bar.

I was elated. I had done the thing that was taboo for women. Lone women in bars are viewed as touting for business, or alcoholics. Why else would they be there? Perish the thought that they might just be enjoying themselves on their own.

As I did this more and more, I noticed that people assumed that I was waiting for someone. I even started to act like I was, periodically looking round at the door in between sips of wine. It took the self-conscious pressure out of the situation.

It was crucial that I only had one drink. Any more, and I would look and feel like an alcoholic. The trick was to make it classy. Sweep in, sit by the bar, exchange pleasantries with the bar staff, look like you're doing some work or going through your emails, finish your one drink, pay up, walk out and hold your head high.

But I was enjoying it too much and as time went on, I'd have two glasses of wine or maybe even three or four, if I got talking to someone. I even had one or two glasses bought for me by women congratulating me on what I was doing. They'd return to their partners and point me out. "Isn't that incredible?" I heard one woman say.

Whilst dealing with the gaslighter at work, I'd started to drink more to alleviate the stress and I wasn't the only one in the company desperate for a bottle of wine at the end of the working day. We even started to call a nearby bar 'the office' because we were there so often. In the daytime, we were all addicted to Diet Coke, to keep us alert enough to deal with the trauma.

One day, I had the idea that I could split my evenings into two: two bites of the cherry. I would have a lovely civilised dinner or drinks with a friend, say goodbye, go home to my flat, and go out again on my own. Why couldn't I do that?

A few months after my last Dahab trip, I was out for dinner on a Saturday night with my friend Chelsea and I decided to try it. She had partied hard in her youth like most of my friends, and was content with going home early. But I didn't want the evening to end there.

Back in my flat, I put music on, poured another glass of

wine and danced in my kitchen, having an internal conversation with myself about whether or not I had the balls to go clubbing on my own. Of course I did – I'd been drinking.

I changed outfits into a sexy, long, black tube dress with a mini denim jacket to cover my arms and boobs. Sexy but not too flesh-baring.

Paradise by Way of Kensal Green, a club, was two minutes down the road from my flat. Ironically for me, this club is named after a line in a GK Chesterton poem, *The Rolling English Road*, in which he advocates middle-aged temperance, lest we '*stretch the folly of our youth to be the shame of age*'. I was definitely stretching mine.

My plan was to go to Paradise and blend in, as best a fortysomething could do in a club filled with people half her age. I'd pretend I was there to meet friends that I had lost in the multi-storeyed, nook-and-crannied building. I couldn't find them, I'd say to anyone who asked.

But first I had to negotiate the bouncers at the door. They must have seen me coming: a woman in her late forties, slightly wobbly, trying not to be wobbly, playing on her phone and pretending to locate her phantom friends. One of the bouncers looked down at me. "Good evening, my love, are you on your own?" he asked, probably knowing the answer to that question.

"No – my friends are already here." I gestured with my head towards the wooden door behind him.

He stared at me for what seemed like minutes but was probably seconds. "And what have you been doing while they've been in there?" he questioned.

"I've been hiking," I said.

It was unexpected enough to sound plausible, because it was often the truth. He gestured me in.

I felt a bit stupid lining up for my wrist stamp but as I

moved towards the bar and the music got louder, I stopped feeling self-conscious. I was in and more white wine was waiting for me.

I pushed my way between the press of bodies and found my way upstairs to the room with the dance floor. I would find a space deep within it and dance until the early hours of the morning.

My wine sloshed over my hands and forearms as I tried to keep my glass aloft between the other dancers. Finally, I found a tiny space next to the raised stage where the DJ was housed. No one would even notice me there. I turned my gaze down, held my glass up to save what was left of the wine and swayed to the music. I was giddy with the thought that I was here alone ... and the wine.

I was facing away from the stage but I sensed I was being watched by someone behind me. It felt as though someone was dancing with me but I was scared to look round in case I saw someone I didn't like. I was enjoying the anonymity of the moment.

It went on, this sightless dancing, and I wondered how long it would last before one of us broke. I twisted my body round to take a peek, and in one choreographed move, a hand reached down to help me up onto the stage. I looked up and it was the last person I ever expected to see – a bearded hipster.

I'd known for a long time that this was not my demographic. Every time I visited East London I felt completely invisible to any men there. They were skinny, bearded and too invested in their own selves to notice anyone else.

I didn't understand this particular world of young men – they were not like Sam or Preston. I always thought that if I so much as placed my body near a hipster boy, I would somehow break his – they always looked so fragile. And yet here was one, pulling me up next to him on stage at Paradise, and offering to hold my wine while I removed my denim jacket. He even tied it around his own waist, so that I wouldn't be troubled by it any further.

He had a dimpled smile in a face I could now take a closer look at. Dark eyes, slicked back dark brown hair, close-cropped beard. He was wearing skinny jeans and a fitted shirt that showed off his long, lean body.

I can't remember asking him to come back to my flat but I did. On the way there I discovered that his name was Hakim. He wasn't a hipster at all – he was Algerian – a Muslim. He was thirty-two.

I felt my stomach flip with a familiar fear. He was North African and Muslim like Sherif, but I hadn't met any Algerians until then. He'd not been drinking when we met but I certainly had. Was it my ridiculous racism again? After all, I'd been happy enough to take a hipster home with me.

I snapped myself out of it as much as I could through the wine haze. In the lift to my floor, we looked at each other properly in the bright light and laughed. Hakim's face was impishly cute when he smiled and his dark eyes sparkled. He looked a little nervous in my presence, not having alcohol to help him through the awkwardness.

Hakim kissed me on my sofa and gently stroked my back. No rushing things for him. I unbuttoned his white shirt and found that his slim torso was covered in dark hair. I wanted to bury my face in it.

He stood up, offering his hand once again, this time to take me to my bedroom.

The next morning, I watched him pull on his shirt and skinny jeans and grinned at my very good luck at pulling someone who was so beautiful on my first solo-clubbing attempt. I guessed I'd probably never see him again, even when he said he'd like to see me. I was used to not expecting anything from these men – it was best not to.

Later that day, I received a text: *"It was lovely to meet you, Lisa, and I hope we will meet again, tomorrow night, if you want to. Let me know. Xxx"*

I was so unused to hearing back from a guy the next day, let alone the same day, wanting to see me again so soon. I tried to wait a suitable amount of time before responding – I think I managed half an hour by distracting myself with housework.

The following evening was a long time coming. This time there was no wine involved. I was fresh from a bath and wrapped in my favourite kimono to receive him. Hakim was wearing skinny jeans, a fitted jumper and a pea coat with a scarf, his hair slicked back. *It must be the French influence*, I thought. He was so stylish. I commented on it.

"Zara," he said.

We sat on my sofa and chatted for a while, drinking water. He'd bought a shrinkwrapped pack of six bottles for my fridge, marvelling that I didn't already have any in there.

"I drink tap water," I said and he looked horrified. I guessed it was a North African thing.

Instead of getting right to it, Hakim wanted to know about my day – what I had been doing (thinking about him mainly) and if I was ok after Saturday night. I was.

After leaving my flat on Sunday morning, he had been with his friends at Westfield in Shepherds Bush. He referred to it as 'The Bush' and I told him he might want to rethink that term. "The locals call it *She-Bu*," I joked and he said it back to me in his French-Arabic accent.

I loved the way he talked – long French vowel sounds alongside harder Arabic consonants. He told me he spoke both languages and later, when I heard him on the phone to one of his friends, I could hear him switching between French, Arabic and English. These guys always put us monoglots to shame. I can't even speak Welsh – my own language.

Hakim was part of a group of Algerian guys who met in a coffee shop just outside Westfield every night, he said. They were all ages, unrelated, just united by their nationality. The framily again.

"Hello you," he said, suddenly looking at me intensely, smiling at me with that all-teeth-pressed-together grin.

He leant forward and kissed me softly again, parting my kimono with one hand. I didn't know what he was going to do next, which I loved. Not knowing what was going to happen was thrilling – like those very first dates with Patrick.

I was used to British men never wanting to hold my hand during sex, perhaps afraid that it would signify that they – shock horror – 'liked' me. If our hands accidentally touched they'd pull back quickly. Their penis was allowed to push inside my vagina but perish the thought that their actual hands would hold mine. And here was Hakim the Algerian holding my hands as he kissed me passionately and pushed deeply into me. It was what I'd been craving since Sherif.

A routine developed with Hakim. He'd see his friends after work – he worked at Heathrow – and then come to mine for about 9 or 10pm, two or three times a week. He always stayed over and the relationship felt like it was progressing, even though I'd never seen him in daylight. I started to refer to myself jokingly as Nighttime Girlfriend.

I loved how Hakim would want to talk about my day before anything physical happened between us. We spent more and more time on the sofa, sometimes cuddled up watching TV. It turned out that he liked natural-history documentaries (what guy doesn't?) and ... Disney movies.

On the day of his birthday, Hakim brought cake to my flat. For me. It was an Algerian tradition – buying cakes for others on your birthday. *How refreshingly generous*, I thought, biting into the sickly sweet butter icing.

Afterwards, we went to a local Moroccan restaurant for dinner and Hakim ordered for me in Arabic. We drank tea rather than wine. I loved being out with him in the outside world, even if it was still dark. I had joked about being Nighttime Girlfriend but I secretly longed to be Daytime Girlfriend too. I was sick of being someone's secret lover; the novelty had worn off.

I asked Hakim what he would do if we bumped into any of his friends when out in public. "Nothing," he said. "It's not a problem."

But I still wondered. He liked to visit me under cover of darkness – would he want to see me in broad daylight?

It transpired that much of the Algerian group had secret Western girlfriends whom they only saw under cover of darkness. Hakim said that this was how it was with all his friends – they only saw women at night. Daytime was for men. It was his normal; it was what everyone did. But it wasn't my normal. I was being kept a secret and I wanted to date someone openly.

Hakim seemed happy to agree to a date on Hampstead Heath when I challenged him about daylight dating. "We'll go for a walk," I said. "And maybe stop for tea and cake?" I wanted to hold his hand in public and be proud of walking next to my tall, handsome, well-dressed man.

He stayed with me one Saturday night and we went walking the next day. He told me he'd been due to meet the

Algerian gang in Westfield that morning, but he'd chosen to be with me instead. I was delighted.

I was a regular weekend hiker at this point in my life, having joined a few groups, and used to walking long distances, fast. Hakim wasn't. He'd laugh incredulously when I said I was going on a fourteen- or eighteen-mile hike. "You will walk all the way home to Wales one day!" he'd joke. This was entirely possible.

Hakim couldn't understand my urge to walk anywhere. I wore sturdy boots to walk on the Heath – Hakim wore suede pointy shoes and his classic pea coat. We walked – very slowly – to my favourite spot on the Heath: Kenwood House. As we neared the tearoom, Hakim bent down and said "Hello!" to a small dog that was trotting towards us. *Could this guy be any more perfect?* I thought.

We chose slices of cake from the vast array at Kenwood tearoom. I sat proudly with my gorgeous man as he daintily sipped his tea from a floral cup and got cake crumbs in his beard. This was the coffee-shop date I'd dreamed of, and here was a man who knew how to linger over a hot drink. After all, he did it for hours with his friends.

We were becoming closer and closer, even though our daylight dates were few and far between. We seemed to work better at night, and Hakim was always busy with his friends during daylight hours. If he wasn't rushing to have coffee with them after work, he was going to Hyde Park with them to play football. But he liked to spend his nights pretending that we were a couple.

I tried to ignore the fact that I was playing second fiddle to the Algerian gang and be happy that I had Hakim in my life at all. Friends checked in with me to make sure that I knew what I was doing. I was being the secret '*haram*' lover of a Muslim man ('forbidden' in Arabic). Yes, yes, I knew. I told myself that lovers were the way forward. Conventional relationships just didn't work out for me.

At Christmas in 2015, I took Hakim to the whitest, most middle-class event of all – the light display at Kew Gardens. He met me in his pea coat outside Kew station and we walked down to the entrance gate with our tickets.

Once I had to explain everything to him – from the Twelve Days of Christmas to Santa's Grotto – it all seemed like complete madness. What even were 'four calling birds' and who needed 'three French hens'? What was an elf? We both laughed. When you stand outside someone else's cultural traditions, they all look a bit ridiculous. But still, he loved the toasted marshmallows and dips – sweet things always went down well with Hakim.

---

I was having a difficult time at work again, in my new job as a publisher back in children's books. For the first six months it was fine, until my first commission came in and without even taking a breath, a colleague claimed that the idea had been hers. The lie was so brazen it took my breath away.

By the end of that first year, I was hiding all the new ideas coming through my team, to the point where we cleared our desks and screens at the end of every day. We knew that she came in early to minesweep our desks in what we called her 'dawn raids'. If anything good was left out, we knew she would lay claim to it immediately and share it with senior management. She kept making up stories about me and my team that I'd be constantly fighting to refute. Once again, the strain of dealing with a toxic person at work started to take a physical toll on me. And led me to the pub.

Hakim cared about how I was coping with it all. He stayed with me for a few nights in a row one week and I joked about him trying to move in. It did not go down well. I didn't see him for a few weeks after that. Either he was horrified that I thought he was trying to worm his way into my flat or I'd hit the nail on the head. I couldn't rid myself of the idea that he was after something more than just me.

I remember Hakim picking small fights over nothing here and there when his feelings were obviously getting stronger. The fights triggered a short separation which would reset the boundaries between us. He once sent me a cute picture of a dog in a jumper because he knew I'd like it and when I said it reminded me of him in his Zara cream jumper, he reacted badly. I looked it up online and found that Muslims consider dogs to be dirty and not worthy of attention. It didn't square with the people I knew in Dahab who loved the dogs there, or Hakim saying hello to one on the Heath.

Early in 2016, Hakim started warning me about Ramadan which would take place in May that year. He would not be allowed to see me for one whole month, and probably for a few weeks before, too. Observant Muslims were supposed to cleanse themselves ahead of the event.

Great. I was the unclean.

However, I was keen to be culturally sympathetic and cool about it all, so I agreed to wait. He could speak to me, or text, but we couldn't see each other. Only married people could have sex during Ramadan, and then only when the sun disappeared.

Waiting to see Hakim over Ramadan was painful. He banned me from texting him in the end because our conversations always got too sexy and he couldn't bear it.

I started googling '*Muslim boyfriend*' and found forums

where people asked questions about what they could and couldn't do during Ramadan. Someone always said, *"He will never be your boyfriend or husband if you are not Muslim – what you are doing is against the Quran and he will ultimately leave you because of his duty to Allah."* I searched for stories where the relationship had worked out – only, it seemed, if the non-Muslim party converted to the faith.

I went to Westfield one day, subconsciously hoping to see Hakim, and there he was, like I'd summoned him, sitting alone on a bench in the mall. He looked surprised to see me. I was wearing a strappy tube dress with a brightly coloured bra underneath. He looked me up and down.

We chatted for a few minutes, but Hakim suddenly made an excuse to leave – he was meeting friends to prepare that night's Iftar meal, he said – and rushed away from me.

Minutes later I received a text. He said he could not be seen with me in public during Ramadan, especially when I was dressed like that. He hoped I understood.

Yeah, I understood. I was his big, dirty, whorish secret.

I waited for the first day of Eid, where I was sure that Hakim would rush round to my flat, eager to jump into my bed. But he didn't. He didn't appear at all for days. The thought entered my head: is he weaning himself off me? I didn't text him – I waited for him to contact me. The silence stretched on for two weeks.

Eventually I caved in and messaged him. *"Are we over? It seems like we are."*

A message returned seconds later: *"No, no, I just need some time for myself. I hope you are ok."*

I knew Hakim was struggling to reconcile me with his faith. And I think I always knew which one would win. I waited until I'd had a few drinks after work a month or so later to challenge him for a second time: "*Are we over now? I think we are. You haven't contacted me in weeks. Please just tell me.*"

"*I can't see you anymore. After I saw you at Westfield, I thought it. It made me think.*"

"*Seeing me in a sexy dress?*"

"*Yes. It didn't make me feel good about myself.*"

"*Well, it didn't make me feel good either. Why didn't you tell me then? Instead, you have kept me waiting for you. All this time after Ramadan.*"

"*I'm sorry. I wanted to tell you.*"

I was distraught, fuelled by wine, and called Hakim's phone over and over again, begging him to talk to me. He wouldn't pick up, even though he clearly had his phone in his hand.

He had two phones and I called both numbers. I think one was his Algerian phone and the other a UK one. Did he have two phones because he was living two lives? No matter, because he answered neither. I left emotional voice-mails pleading with him not to end it. In the end I resorted to a last text to make my feelings known. He had not been known to prioritise my sexual pleasure over his own...

"*When you get your next girlfriend, you might want to make sure that she doesn't have to get herself off while you're in the shower.*"

A text came back: it was the crying laughing-face emoji.

———

I swore off men after that. I'd tried everything – a husband, other people's husbands, younger men, men my age, and more recently, Muslim men.

Hakim and I had lasted two years – longer than any

relationship I'd had since my marriage – but was it really a relationship?! I'd always known it would end – how could it not? – but it hurt more than I thought it would. I knew he'd be hurting too. Hakim had cared for me deeply and shown it on many occasions. But I had been disappointed in only being Nighttime Girlfriend and I longed to walk in the daylight, no longer someone's secret.

I stopped looking for men, or even at men. I was sick of them, and sick of needing to be seen and validated by them. I deleted all the dating apps on my phone and stopped going for second nights out, prowling for men. I wanted to just be me for a while, in the world on my own. And I stopped thinking of that as a bad option.

I didn't want to be tethered to a man who kept me hidden away for nighttime use only, and I was slightly horrified that I had allowed that to happen. I loved waking up in my own bed alone, with a coffee and catch-up TV, not having to make sure I had bottles of water in the fridge, constantly rushing for work and washing bodily fluids off my sheets. I seriously started to question whether I needed a man at all.

I was happy with my life as it was – a lovely flat, a good fulfilling job (even with a narcissist), good friends, hiking and solo travel. If I had to factor in a man to all of that it would cramp my style, and I'd already made that mistake with my ex-husband.

Was being alone my destiny? I was starting to think it was. But as soon as a woman says that, people immediately conclude that she is just making the best of her disappointingly single life. I heard myself say the words out loud to friends and even I didn't believe me. Surely, subconsciously, I was hoping that if I acted like I didn't need love at all, then I would find it? It would sneak up on me when I was least expecting it. But no one had ever snapped me up and now I was nearly fifty. There wasn't a demographic interested in me apart from younger men and forbidden men (or both) who just wanted me for sex. Men my age and older were scared off by my professional success, independent life, and feminist opinions.

I came up with a new phrase to describe my current state: I'd evolved past love. I'd evolved past needing it, wanting it, expecting it. (I've since realised I borrowed this from Samantha Jones in *Sex and the City* who evolves past a man who broke her heart and then promptly sleeps with him again years later and regrets it).

I wondered why life had carved this path out for me and thought I was very alone on it. I only started to realise I wasn't alone when I met other women who were literally and metaphorically on the same one.

In my hiking groups, I met women who were just like me. They were around my age – confident, intelligent, childfree (mostly by choice), attractive, adventurous – I'd even go as far as to say 'sparkling'. We'd have the same conversation every time we met. They'd tell me that they'd tried dating men their own age (the rare ones that didn't want to date younger women), but the guys wouldn't be able to keep up with their 'get-up-and-go' or sex drive. The men didn't want to go out and do things as much as they did, so they left them behind to go hiking. It reminded me of a phrase I'd read by Dr Kate Davidson: '*Men want someone to come home to, women want someone to go out with.*' I'd wanted to go out with Hakim but he'd wanted to come 'home' to me. He even called my flat 'home' when he texted to say he was on his way.

These women would tell me that they had their eye on someone a bit older, but then they'd discover that he was dating someone twenty years younger than them, because he could. Like me, these women got quite a lot of interest from younger men, but wanted someone to share a present and a future with. Boys didn't offer much in that way – they were often just after the mature 'sexperience'. We were a bucket-list thing.

And always, always, these conversations ended with a woman sharing a recent experience where she'd been chatting to a guy her age online, but he'd mysteriously disappeared, reappeared, then disappeared again. In search of answers, she'd tell me that these men called her 'scary' or 'out of their league' and I'd nod in agreement. I hear you, sister.

We'd then walk along together, chuckling in solidarity as we watched the guys our age in the group chatting up the young women, ignoring us completely. I'd decided to ignore them long ago. They didn't see me, so I refused to see them. It was liberating – not caring if they were interested or not. I always made eye contact and smiled at other women. They were the ones that mattered in my world. I had found my tribe.

When my fiftieth birthday rolled around in March 2017, I held my party in Paradise by way of Kensal Green, reclaiming the space in which I'd met Hakim. I bought a tight, black-velvet dress from French Connection with a see-through mesh panel down the cleavage.

My party would take place after the first day of London Book Fair, on my actual birthday. From about 4.30pm onwards, the fair would be filled with the sound of popping prosecco bottles so I knew it would be easy for my publishing friends to make their wobbly way from Olympia to the venue.

I went back to my flat early to pour myself several drinks and pour myself into my dress. There was no way I was rocking up to my fiftieth birthday without some sort of prosecco fortification inside me.

The party filled with colleagues, publishing friends and members of my new hiking tribe. I'd had a slight moment of sadness that once again, I had organised and was celebrating a momentous birthday alone, without a man. But if this was 'alone', being surrounded by so many people I loved, I was happy with it. I'd had to organise my own thirtieth and fortieth birthdays so I knew the drill.

It helped that I'd trained my friends to stop saying they hoped I was being 'spoilt rotten' on my birthday. By whom, exactly? What if there was no one there to spoil me? What if the person I was once married to chose to frogmarch me round the nearest shopping centre until I chose an expensive practical item I didn't need or want? I was in charge of spoiling me, so I encouraged my friends to stop thinking someone else was doing it. There were no 'loved ones' at home tending to my every need, but there were loved ones in that room in Paradise.

As I stood in front of the huge rainbow cake bought for me by my friends, wearing my sexy black dress, I addressed the crowd: "I'm standing here brandishing a huge knife with my tits out! Happy 50th birthday to me!"

LIVE

# AGONDA BEACH

## SOUTH GOA, INDIA – DECEMBER 2017

I woke up to the sounds of waves crashing, crows cawing and voices shouting outside my hut. A dog barked and I was sure I'd just heard the low of a cow.

It was 8am. Time for breakfast dress.

I emerged from the front door of my hut and Goa greeted me: golden sand, green-blue ocean with roiling, shining, big waves and dogs curled up like doughnuts in the shade of trees.

Dinesh was grinning at me in the restaurant next to the hut. He was wearing smart chinos and a light-blue shirt. I'd definitely got him out of bed last night. "Did you sleep well?" he said, twinkling. "Did you find the bathroom ok?"

I laughed and found a seat at a wooden table in the shade. It was next to the beach and the breeze blew in. A familiar black dog with a white flash appeared in front of me and stretched out her front paws – Sweetpea! Here she was at last. She let out a little yowl of hello.

"Everybody loves Sweetpea," Dinesh said. "She likes white people because they give her biscuits. She's a bit racist like that."

Sweetpea settled at my feet while I ordered coffee and eggs. I couldn't believe I was there. My coffee mug had '*Goa*' written on it with a beach scene in relief. I lay my *Lonely Planet* travel guide next to it.

To spoil myself rotten in my fiftieth year, I booked a holiday to Goa at Christmas. I wanted to go to somewhere new and far away, as I'd done on that very first trip to Thailand. I decided that I would do it every year, and make Christmas my main holiday. It made sense to make the most of work Christmas holidays and go away when most people were having family time at home. I could do the opposite and have me-time on the other side of the world.

I can't remember exactly how I found Agonda – I think the beach was listed as one of the best in the world on Trip-Advisor. It was a turtle-nesting site, which caught my attention. I loved places in the world with animals. I loved beaches and places where I could wear my breakfast dresses by the sea.

I knew where I would stay almost immediately. Its name was Simrose. It had review after amazing review about its location, its staff, its dog. Its dog! I found Sweetpea immediately on the Simrose Instagram page. She was black with white-tipped paws and a white flash down her nose and chest. She wore a red collar. I would go and spend Christmas with Sweetpea.

India was a scary thought – perhaps even scarier than Egypt had been at first. The scaremongering about it was worse for women – stories flew round about gang rapes and brutal murders. What was I doing, booking a holiday there alone?

But Goa was 'gateway India', I was told by friends who'd been, and not the 'real' India. It was an easier and safer option for a solo woman. But still, I was to be very, very careful at all times, they said.

I emailed Simrose to book a luxury hut right on the beach with a view of the sea and an open-air bathroom. I wanted to treat myself after another stressful year at work, dealing with all the problems caused by the narcissist. Someone called Dinesh responded – I recognised his name from the TripAdvisor reviews. *"The best manager ever!"* they said. I paid a deposit into the Simrose bank account and I was all set. Soon I would meet Sweetpea the dog and we would share the sunset on the beach.

I arrived at Dabolim airport in the middle of the night. As we stood up to disembark, I saw a dog run across the tarmac. *I'm going to like it here*, I thought.

At passport control I discovered the Indian penchant for teasing as I had my fingerprint scan. I have short ring fingers on both my hands (a genetic thing) and struggled to place those fingers on the scanner.

"I'm sorry, madam, we can't let you in," the official said with a straight face.

For one millisecond, I believed him. He grinned.

I was met outside by Nagesh, my Simrose driver, wearing a white shirt and trousers and an even whiter smile. He was holding a sign with my name on it. I grinned back and waved as I walked into the wave of heat, men all around shouting, "Taxi, taxi!" with dogs weaving between their legs.

Nagesh was young and handsome with an undercut in his hair and a short ponytail on top – his head wobbled as I shook his hand. How I've come to love that Indian head wobble, that seems to say 'hello, yes, everything is ok, I'm very happy to meet you' all in one.

Dogs were sleeping along the side of the road as we

walked to the airport car park, sometimes lying in the middle of it. I gabbled nervously about them – Nagesh didn't even seem to notice their presence.

As we drove out of the airport he negotiated cows, dogs, tuktuks, cars and people. All in a day's work, it seemed. I couldn't see much out of the windows that night but we drove through various towns where dogs seemed to be in charge while the humans were asleep. They continued sleeping in the middle of the road while Nagesh manoeuvred around them.

Finally, we turned into a gateway where I could just make out a carved wooden sign that said 'Simrose'. I was there! It might have been 2.30am but I was actually there. And there was the manager, Dinesh, ready to meet me. As soon as he opened the car door, I could hear the waves. "Is that sound real?!" I asked incredulously.

"It's the waves!" he said, smiling, gesturing for me to follow him. "They are louder at night."

He was wearing a T-shirt and shorts – had he got out of bed to meet me? If he had, he seemed cheery about it. He showed me to my beach hut – my bag had already got there, somehow. The walls and all the furniture were made from the same dark wood. There was a four-poster bed with mosquito-net curtains all around it, and embroidered cushions on the white bed. There was a painted dark-wood wardrobe, chest of drawers and a bamboo coat stand in the corner.

"As you've booked a hut with no bathroom," said Dinesh, "I'd advise you to get up at around 5.30am to queue for the shower and toilet."

I stared at him. I was pretty sure that when I'd viewed the hut on the Simrose website it came with an open-air bathroom. In the milliseconds that followed, I'd already come to terms with the information and started working out how I'd cope.

Then I spotted the door in the back corner of the room. "Where does that go?" I enquired, pointing at it.

"To the outside," Dinesh answered quickly.

Silence. Apart from my brain whirring at the inconvenience, but being too jetlagged to complain about it.

Dinesh walked over to the door and opened it with a flourish. "Only joking – here is your bathroom!"

I almost fell over with relief. Dinesh showed me how the shower worked and left me to go back to his own bed. I was left with the sound of the waves – so loud! No one mentioned how loud they would be in the reviews – and I couldn't get to sleep. But oh, how marvellous, being there, in India, by the sea. And somewhere outside my hut was a dog called Sweetpea.

That first morning, I watched Dinesh fire off orders to the kitchen staff while I waited for my breakfast. They were all from Nepal, he said, himself included, and worked there ten months of the year, including 'set up' and 'close down' – they were required to dismantle the resort every year because of Indian tourism regulations.

The music in the restaurant kept cutting out and so did the wifi connecting me to the world back home. This was normal service, I would discover quickly. And anyway, no one would be up back in the UK – I was five and a half hours ahead. Perhaps this holiday would offer me some much-needed time away from social media and my smartphone. I was more than a little addicted.

After my traditional coffee and omelette breakfast – this time with masala – I retired to my hut to coat myself in Factor 50 and settle on a sunlounger on my balcony. The doughnut dogs had stretched themselves out and were sitting like miniature sentinels facing the sea. I wondered what they were looking out for.

Unable to resist, I decided to cover up and join them on the beach to walk towards what looked like a river estuary. The whole beach was covered in dogs – some lying in the shade of boats, some sitting in the laps of people trying to meditate on the beach. I was in beach-dog heaven.

Everyone I passed said, "Good morning!" – some were Indian, some tourists. Everyone looked happy and even the dogs appeared to be smiling. Further down the beach, fishermen were pulling in large nets from the water, filled with a silvery catch, shouting at each other in what I later found out was Konkani – the official language of Goa. Their wooden boats were white, edged with distressed blue and brown paint. They had wooden struts extended on one side, to balance the boats in the waves, like a catamaran.

I reached the river and could see the trees on the other bank moving – monkeys! There they were – light blonde with dark faces, swinging around, putting on a morning show for me. The river bent round to my right and I could see more fishing boats lying on the sand. Sea eagles flew high overhead and long-legged sand plovers hopped into the water next to me. Tiny crabs disappeared into pre-dug holes in front of my feet as I walked on. There was a bridge in the distance and tuktuks and people on scooters were going over it. This was India!

I walked back to my sunlounger as the sun beat down on my Celtic skin – I would sit out the hottest hours of the day in the shade and read books. I'd found, in the last few years, that my brain couldn't settle enough to read anything at home. Maybe it was social media and internet browsing that had made it restless, maybe it was the stress of managing a busy team at work with a hovering narcissist –

but whatever it was, I could only really read for pleasure on holiday.

It was Christmas Eve and I was sitting in front of my hut overlooking the beach, with a book in my hand, and another dog, Jerry, at my feet. He also belonged to Simrose – he was old and going blind but that didn't stop him getting up to bark at intermittent intervals.

Christmas in Agonda is, I discovered, very special. It is a unique blend of Catholic and Hindu festivity. The beach huts at Simrose had large paper stars in different colours hanging from their roofs. My hut had a white star that lit up as the rosy sun set below the sea. It looked like the manger in the nativity scenes of my childhood advent calendars. It had strings of small round mirrors dangling from its roof; they reflected the sunlight by day and the starlight by night. I put my book down and looked out at the neverending horizon in the magenta haze of twilight. I wanted to sail into it and never stop.

I spent Christmas Day in much the same way, although my peace was disturbed by the sound of families in the restaurant next to my hut, recreating the Xmas they would normally have at home. They had brought party hats and crackers – exactly the sort of thing I was coming here to get away from.

I snuck out of my hut to eat a non-Christmas lunch of chicken xacuti in the restaurant, sitting in one of the Simrose 'cabanas' – large four-poster wooden structures with low-seating and jewel-coloured cushions. There were bowls of water outside each one, and all the huts, for washing the sand off your feet before going in barefoot.

At around 4pm, everyone on the beach watched in delight as two herds of cows gathered there – one on each side of Simrose. Even the dogs reappeared in their sentinel positions to monitor proceedings.

Dinesh told me that the cows, which were wild and sacred, were fed at the same time every day. They were given leftovers from the Simrose kitchen and the resort next door. If they got too hungry they would try and eat things they weren't supposed to – screams and laughter had mingled when one of them tried to steal a tourist's paperback book earlier that day.

Two of the kitchen hands ran out through the restaurant and down onto the beach carrying a wooden box, sedan-chair style, covered in black plastic. They raced between the two groups of cows, plonked the box down and whipped off the plastic covering. They needed to be quick – the cows were powerful and dangerous when they were hungry.

I had walked the length and breadth of the beach a few times in the first three days, but I still hadn't ventured out of Simrose into the town. It had taken time and courage to go into Patong, Bodrum and Dahab on my own – and by now I'd added Tamarindo in Costa Rica to that list – but it always turned out well.

By the time Boxing Day came around, I'd started to get literal cabin fever in my beautiful hut. I decided that after breakfast, I would venture out. I donned my customary long skirt and covered my shoulders with a scarf – quite apart from respecting the local culture, I was scared of getting really, really burned by the sun. I'd been horribly roasted in Kenya and in Costa Rica, thinking I could go without suncream under an umbrella. I'd spent days inside as a result, smothered in aloe vera. That would not be happening here.

I walked through the Simrose gardens, past all the other

huts and the main guest house where I waved at Malika and Manish on reception. I walked down the drive towards the main gates and saw cows crossing in front of them. I walked out on to the road and narrowly avoided a family of three on a scooter.

I walked out into a street filled with colour and life. Portuguese-style villas were painted bright green, turquoise blue and vivid red, and festooned with tinsel and paper stars. By the church next to Simrose there was a gathering of tuktuks and scooters – their drivers offering to take me to nearby Palolem or Patnem.

I could hear singing coming from the church – the familiar sound of Catholic mass taking place. The huge white and blue façade of the church had a cerise pink awning erected outside it so that people could sit in the shade if they couldn't fit inside. There was a school adjoining the church with a beachside playground.

I couldn't believe it had taken me this long to walk through magical Agonda. It was one long strand of shops, restaurants and cafés with painted wooden signs indicating beachside venues, and carts selling masala chai. There were stalls selling fresh fruit and vegetables, spices and every sort of tea. Next to one, there was a family of piglets squealing, and cows were everywhere, lounging in the shade. Dogs walked along the street as though they had somewhere to be – they acted like they were part of the community as they had in Bodrum and Dahab. I loved it.

A small Indian woman wearing a lime-green tunic and red leggings called out to me. "Good morning! See something you like? I give you good price!"

The young woman's name was Gita and she owned two of the clothes shops on the main street with her husband, Manu. I looked through the racks of dresses and wanted one in every colour. They had metallic threads running through them and I was a sucker for shiny things. I selected two – in blue and purple – both with gold thread. I wanted to shimmer in Goa, especially at breakfast. I was unsure of the value of the rupees I was paying Gita, but I was so happy to be out and about in India I would have paid anything.

As I walked back to Simrose, giddy with my first purchases, I spotted a bar that opened on to the street. It had an open roof fringed with what looked like straw, tiki-style, and I could see the staff busying themselves with preparation for the day and night ahead. There was an open kitchen to one side, with a large pizza oven in front of it. A carved wooden sign told me that this was '*Kopi Desa*' (Indonesian for 'coffee village', I later found out, although they seemed to serve everything *but* coffee).

I was so happy with my new dresses – hanging them up next to all my international breakfast dresses on my bamboo coat stand. I would wear one of them that night to go to Kopi Desa.

As I'd done in Thailand all those years before, I had a few cocktails in the resort bar before I ventured out that evening. I couldn't eat dinner because I was too nervous. I was great at going to bars on my own, but I'd never done it in India.

When I arrived at Kopi Desa, all the bar stools were full, mainly with tourists. I couldn't just stand around – I'd stand out too much – so I ventured inside and found more stools to sit on. I ordered a cocktail.

Immediately, a British guy loomed into my space. "May I join you?" he asked in a Brummie accent. I didn't really have a choice but at least he would be a distraction in this busy bar. He was about my age, dark-haired with a drooping moustache. He was drunk. He talked at me about his travels in India for about ten minutes before saying he needed the loo.

I looked up, taking a sip of my elderflower and prosecco fizz, and saw an older British couple gesturing at me. "Are you ok?" they mouthed at me. I shook my head and they beckoned me over. "He's been hitting on women all day," they said. They'd rescued a few, it seemed. "Come and join us," they added, so I did, figuring Dennis from Birmingham might not even notice that I'd moved. He didn't even try and join us when he returned from the toilet.

I talked to Dave and Lynn from Berkshire and they said they'd been coming to Kopi Desaturate for a week or so and couldn't believe how great it was. Dave put his hand on my arm. "Let me introduce you to The Most Handsome Man in Goa!" he said, gesticulating at the barman who was hovering behind us.

I'd noticed him earlier – taller than most of the staff, with a beard and bushy hair. His nickname was Shaggy – real name, Shubham. The manager of the bar was also called Shubham. It was very confusing.

The Most Handsome Man in Goa grinned shyly at me. He had the looks of a Bollywood star and I felt sure that he was one of those guys who had a different woman every night and played the tourists hard during the season. But when I spoke to him, I discovered that he had a slight stammer and he giggled a lot, showing a fetching gap in his front teeth. He taught me how to say his name properly and said that most British people got it wrong, but I hadn't. His name meant 'lucky' in Sanskrit.

We grinned at each other every time he walked past, every time he shook his cocktail shaker and every time he looked around for the next customer to serve. *My oh my*, I thought, but I wasn't here for that. Not this time. This was the holiday that would be man-free. Except I kept going back to Kopi Desa that week after Christmas and I kept buying sparkly sexy dresses from Gita to wear in the evenings.

Every time evening rolled round, I couldn't resist a couple of cocktails at Simrose and then a slow walk round to Kopi, looking forward to the moment that Shubham would spot me coming, or when the other barmen would call his name, seeing me coming down the road.

Shubham was twenty-five and he lived in Palolem with his parents. He had four sisters. You can always tell when a man has been raised around lots of women – for one thing he's not scared of someone like me, and for another, he treats women with respect.

I started going earlier and earlier to the bar, until by the end of that week I was arriving there before sunset and fore-going Simrose sundowners and the cow feeding on the beach. I wanted to pull up a stool in front of Shubham and get him to giggle and show the gap in his white teeth. I wanted to get him to look at me with the huge dark eyes that lurked under his thick black eyebrows.

He had an adorable habit of saying, "And what...?" when the conversation stopped, like he wanted something else to happen. I liked Shubham. But at the end of each night, I would bid him goodnight and go back to my hut at Simrose.

During that 'Twixtmas' week, I got to know a couple of people who were staying in Agonda for the season: Chris, a British guy with a freelance marketing business and Guru, an Indian from Delhi who was there for the yoga and the partying. The two of them appeared to have made friends with everyone in sight and I was quickly drawn into their group. It gave me an excuse to go to the bar even more often, but not just sit there talking to Shubham.

New Year's Eve was approaching and Guru was planning a party in his rooms across the road from the bar. He had a balcony and we would have full view over the town. I had located an off-licence selling the all-important sparkling wine, so I bought a couple of bottles to take along. Shubham and the Kopi boys were planning to go to the hotel bar next to theirs after closing time and Shubham shyly suggested that he might meet me there to celebrate New Year. I was delighted.

I'd been telling myself that this holiday wasn't about a man, that I was just enjoying this guy's company. I told myself that he was too good-looking, too young, and he wouldn't be interested in me. But as the days went on, I could see that he looked forward to seeing me and I couldn't miss a day seeing him. I'd already wasted three days before getting out of Simrose and I wasn't going to waste any more.

---

*It's early on New Year's Eve and I'm in my hut. The power is flicking on and off, as per usual between 6pm and 7pm, when everyone is trying to use it. I pull my hair up into a top knot and put on one of my sparkly halterneck dresses from Gita's stall. Dinesh offers me a cocktail at the Simrose bar so I decide to have one for Dutch courage – caipirowska, please. I swish out of Simrose with my sparkling wine fresh from the fridge, and head to Guru's party.*

*When I arrive, he is high above me on his balcony, beckoning me to come up, surrounded by a throng of people. He has placed jars containing candles on either side of the steps leading up to his rooms, and they flicker across the balcony as I am introduced to everyone.*

*I am handed a champagne glass filled with sparkling wine and I can't believe I'm here. Guru and Chris's friends are from all over the world and all much younger than me. No matter – they don't care. We are all ecstatic that we are here, on New Year's Eve.*

*I am looking down on a scene filled with noise and light – paper stars, tinsel and the sound of cows and dogs barking, scooters revving their engines and beeping their horns, people shouting. The world is alight and alive.*

*As it approaches midnight, Guru and Chris hatch an alternative plan to head to nearby Palolem for New Year. No!!! I am determined to meet Shubham in Agonda.*

*I head out by myself, filled with alcohol-fuelled courage, knowing that if there is one thing I can do, it's go for a second night out by myself. I walk into H2o – the resort next to Kopi Desa – and it's packed with revellers around the bar. I plunge into the three-people-deep throng and waste some time getting myself set up with more sparkling wine. It's 11.15pm.*

*I slosh some wine onto the sand as I step down on to the beach in front of the resort. People are standing around waiting for the fireworks at midnight, faces lit by torch flame.*

*A British couple smile at me and beckon me over. Lucy and Jason – they are on their honeymoon round-the-world trip. They ask me about why I'm here and I fill them in on a bit of my 'journey'. I tell them about Shubham and that I'm hoping to meet him here at midnight. They know him – they've met him at the bar. "The really handsome one with the beard," Lucy says.*

*Yes. That's him. They get almost excited as me about the*

prospect. We clink glasses and wait in the sand for everything to start.

I keep looking behind me but as the fireworks begin at midnight, Shubham is nowhere to be seen.

I make the most of the party with Lucy and Jason, dancing in the sand, letting wine splash over my hands. Getting drunk.

Jason offers to go and get myself and Lucy some more wine and we carry on dancing.

Perhaps I've imagined the whole thing with Shubham. Maybe he is, after all, just another guy in a bar chatting up women of a certain age for entertainment. He's probably gone to Palolem.

"Lisa!" I hear Jason shout from the back of the hotel lounge. "Lisa! Look who's here!"

I turn around and there is a gap-toothed grin coming towards me. There is no sign of the other Kopi boys – they've gone to Palolem. But he has come here. To me.

Shubham pulls the rucksack off his back and out comes a bottle of sparkling wine and two glasses. Is he allowed to do that in another bar? Why do I care?

Lucy and Jason have disappeared into the night and I am here with him: The Most Handsome Man in Goa. We are sitting on the sand and he is pouring me a glass of wine and we are grinning stupidly at each other.

"Sorry I missed midnight," he says, and I tell him it's fine.

"And what...?"

And what ... is getting on the back of Shubham's bike and heading back to my hut at Simrose, not caring if the staff can see us.

And what ... is letting his soft lips kiss me and putting my hands in his thick black hair. Finally.

*And what ... is waking up next to him in the morning and looking into his eyes.*

*It is the best New Year's Day morning I've ever had, as he kisses me, strokes me, makes me come hard. He has to rush off to work and doesn't bother about himself. That's new...*

*Shubham has to do a walk of shame through Simrose back to his bike. I wonder if it bothers him as much as it bothers me, as find it difficult to look Dinesh in the eye at breakfast.*

*And what...?*

---

Every day in Agonda, I witnessed a white horse walking up and down the beach, slowly, on her own, calling into various establishments for water. I discovered that she walked through the town every morning and every evening, to and from wherever she lived. At sunset, she stopped frequently at the water's edge as if posing for Instagram shots, and then called into Kopi Desa for water on her way back.

No one knew to whom she belonged, if she belonged to anyone. She was just White Horse. I decided that White Horse was my spirit animal. Hell, we even frequented the same bar. For me, she embodied freedom. We walked alone because we wanted to. But what about The Most Hand-some Man in Goa? Didn't I want to walk with him?

I walked the seashore alone in the mornings and evenings and went for bike rides with Shubham to hidden beaches during the day. He told me I was free to do what I wanted, that I wasn't tethered to him. Initially I thought he was keeping his options open, but it became clear that he wanted me to feel free, just like White Horse.

The night I left Goa, I visited Kopi for the last time,

knowing I'd be getting a taxi to the airport at 10.30pm. I had more cocktails with Chris and Guru than I'd planned and I felt the tears well up inside me.

That morning, I'd done a yoga class with Lucia, an Italian yoga teacher who taught at Simrose. She warned us that we might feel emotional afterwards, because we'd focused on heart-opening poses. I dismissed the idea until a wellspring of emotion bubbled up at the bar that evening, fuelled by sparkling wine. Shubham could see the waves breaking inside me and sprang from behind the bar, offering to drive me back to Simrose on his scooter. I'd already packed but I sobbed as I changed out of my beach dress into my travel outfit.

"Don't cry, don't cry," he said as he held my head in his hands and wiped the tears away with his thumbs. I was inconsolable.

Nagesh was ready in the car as we wheeled my suitcase out of my hut and Shubham lifted it into the boot. I couldn't kiss him goodbye in public and I felt my heart exploding in my chest. As the car drew away, I saw Shubham speed away on his bike not even looking back. He was upset too. I sobbed.

"Madam, control yourself!" Nagesh cried from the front of the car, trying to console me in his own way. But I continued to cry as I walked into the airport and into the queue for check-in.

In Goa, I had glimpsed something very special and I knew I needed to experience it again. It wasn't just the attention of The Most Handsome Man in Goa, but something more essential.

I had started to observe a personal ritual. It was like the rising and the setting of the sun: an early morning walk on the beach, saying hello to the doughnut dogs, a yoga class that reminded me of the dance classes I'd loved as a young woman, the donning of a new breakfast dress and a retreat to my sunlounger where I read and read until the cows gathered on the beach for their daily feed. White Horse would come along, right on schedule, to signal the ending of the day and the beginning of a night filled with joy and passion.

Before I left, Dinesh had said, "You are part of the Simrose family now."

I felt it. I really felt it. Not just the sales line of a very good manager to his customer, but something more.

The place had been full of returning guests and I could see why. It wasn't the most luxurious place on the beach but the staff there made everyone feel like they were home. And Sweetpea the dog completed the picture.

Guru and Chris joked that I had 'Agonda Fever'. Its victims always return ... again and again.

On my return to the UK in January 2018, I immediately joined an online yoga community with unlimited webcam classes. I was determined to keep the momentum going on my newly discovered routine. I'd always thought yoga wasn't 'real' exercise until those classes in Goa – and I didn't believe in anything like chakras until my heart had opened up on that last day.

Being in a webcam class suited me – I couldn't see anyone else, just the teacher, so I couldn't compare myself negatively with other people and back out. I kept it going until I returned to Simrose the following Christmas.

All through that year, I stayed in touch with Shubham via WhatsApp and Facebook. We videomessaged, as I'd done with Sherif in Egypt, and the signal was always terrible. We grinned at each other and said, "And what…?"

I booked to go back for three weeks over Christmas and New Year. It would be a long wait but worth it to get such a long break at the end of it. But in April, Shubham broke the news that he was going to work on a cruise ship. He would be away over Christmas and New Year and back in April the following year. I was happy for him, to be suddenly going around the world when he had only ever known Goa, but unhappy for me.

But I didn't change my holiday dates – I was fixated on the idea of getting three weeks in India and I couldn't do that at any other time. I would go back and enjoy my time there without Shubham. It would be a shame, but something was pulling me back to Agonda and I knew I wasn't done. I knew this wasn't just about a man and if we were meant to be together, the universe would sort it out.

I always return to places I've visited on my own. The first trip is a reconnaissance mission, often featuring a three-day exclusion zone in the place I'm staying before I pluck up the courage to go outside. Then I find my feet, scoping out the surrounding area for ATMs, breakfast-dress shops and bars, only really relaxing on the last few days, when I have the lie of the land. The second trip gives me the chance to hit the ground running. It feels great to know where everything is, and to know a few people when I go back. In Thailand, Turkey, Egypt, Costa Rica and now India, I'd found my feet and made a return visit to have the holiday I'd intended to have in the first place.

I didn't want my holidays to be determined by men but my many returns to Egypt had been. The fact that Shubham wouldn't be there in Agonda this time began to appeal to me. I would make it a yoga holiday and focus on

myself for a change. Perhaps I would try to eat more health-
ily, drink less (because I wouldn't be frequenting the bar
where Shubham worked) and get up earlier to play with the
dogs on the beach. Yes, I could have a very decent holiday in
Agonda without a man to complicate it.

I expected the messaging with Shubham to die away
over the course of the year as it had done with Sherif, but it
didn't. He messaged me from every port and I eagerly
accepted his videomessage requests, even when I was at
work. "And what...?"

We went over and over the story of how we'd met and
New Year's Eve. He liked to hear me say that Dave had
introduced him as The Most Handsome Man in Goa. It
made him giggle. He liked to recount how Jason had
approached him in H2o on New Year's Eve and told him
that I was waiting for him. We couldn't get enough of telling
each other our origin story. It was like watching the same
romantic movie with him, over and over again.

Before we knew of his cruise-ship plans, we fantasised
about me turning up in Agonda unannounced, walking into
Kopi one night. I dreamt about it – seeing his gap-toothed
grin. If he'd had a tail, Shubham would have wagged it
whenever I walked up to the bar. His grin always showed
how excited he was to see me. There was no hiding his
affection, which I loved. Now we wouldn't get to recreate
that moment, but we always ended every call by saying that
some day, we would meet again. It would happen, if it was
meant to be. Perhaps he would come to London, he joked. I
knew that was unlikely, and I knew he would hate the cold
and grey of my home city. He belonged to the sunshine and
the ocean.

As December neared, I found out that Shubham's ship
would call into Goa a week before I was due to be there.

Thanks, universe. It seemed as though we were destined never to meet again and I took it as a sign. *He's too young anyway*, I thought.

Whenever I pointed out the age gap to Shubham, he got annoyed – he refused to be put off by it. But I knew it would have to be dealt with. As with all my younger lovers, I knew there was an end date on our romance.

I walked back into Kopi on my second night back in Agonda, seeing the smiles of recognition on the faces of my friends, the barmen: Ram, Shubham Two, Wiki and Shushant. I knew they would tell Shubham One that I was there again and I wanted them to tell him that I was on my own. I would not be seeing any other men. And I was also drinking lime and soda. Used to seeing me order cocktail after cocktail, the boys were in shock.

Over the course of the year in between visits, I'd become increasingly aware that my drinking was getting out of control. I was a classic binge-drinker, congratulating myself for not drinking for two or three nights in a row then downing a bottle and a half of prosecco as a 'reward'.

Work was stressful so I looked for and found willing after-work drinks partners to go to the pub with. I was relying on the release afforded by a binge to anaesthetise my brain and stop me having to think about work and life as a solo woman.

For all its freedoms, I still had nagging doubts about the viability of single life for a woman like me. Coupledom is marketed to us everywhere as the default human setting and we're made to think that independent lives are somehow deficient. I'd see my female hiking friends at weekends and we'd congratulate ourselves on our freedom, but then talk about our dating disasters in the pub afterwards. We were all still casting about for partnerships. We'd down several glasses of wine to make up for all the disappointment and not be able to get out of bed the next day.

My entire diary was arranged around recovery times from binges. I couldn't go out for two nights in a row; I couldn't go out on a Monday because it affected my working week too much. And as soon as Wednesday or Thursday came around, I felt the need to reward myself for having got that far through the week without booze. I'd stumble through Thursdays and Fridays in a fug of exhaustion and somehow get myself to a hike again on a Saturday at 8am.

I decided that I would go back to Goa with a different mindset. It wouldn't be a drinking holiday and it wouldn't involve a man (the two always seemed to go together). I would take cues from the yoga lifestyle and try to be more mindful about what I was putting into my body. I wasn't dieting, but I'd lost two stones simply from balancing my calorie intake (eating what I liked) against walking everywhere. I was still walking to and from work and hiking at weekends. I wanted to limit my alcohol intake to keep my weight stable and I didn't want to eat junk food the next day. I started to use an app to track my drinking, as I'd done with food.

A friend from one of my hiking groups was going to be in Agonda at the same time as me that Christmas. Both of us enjoyed a drink. Initially I'd thought, *Great! We can go on a beach bar crawl together!* But as the time grew near I was trying to think of ways to get out of having to drink heavily with her. I didn't want to spoil my holiday by getting drunk all the time. I wanted early mornings walking with the doughnut dogs on the beach and daily early yoga classes.

In August 2018, I started seeing a therapist. I'd had more than five years of stress working in toxic environments and they were taking their toll on my body and mind. Yoga and hiking were helping me cope, but they weren't enough on their own.

I told her about my drinking worries and she didn't comment or pass judgement. Instead, she worked on the possible root causes of the unhappiness I'd carried around for quite some time now, way before my marriage.

The therapist seemed to think it all stemmed back to losing my father at the age of ten to bowel cancer. I thought this narrative was way too reductive – lots of people lose members of their families in much worse circumstances, I said. I was keen to find the 'real' root cause of my unhappiness, not this classic psychotherapist one. I wasn't a cliché.

I hadn't even connected my drinking to my unhappiness until then. I thought it was something that existed completely independently, something that I loved doing and loved doing a little too much. It was a coping mechanism, and I viewed it as an escape from real life. I didn't know then that it was one of the *causes* of the unhappiness.

I noticed that I'd started to become associated with drinking at work and in my hiking groups. "Lisa likes a drink," people started to say. Friends and colleagues bought me cards featuring drinking jokes and bottles of champagne as presents. I joked with them that I could never have 'just one' but never saw it as a problem – it was just 'how I drank'. It annoyed me that some people would warn me before meeting up with me for lunch or dinner that they wouldn't be drinking. I was annoyed that they felt the need to tell me.

Alcohol made me do bad things and make bad choices. Under its influence, I kissed people I shouldn't, and much worse. I didn't feel good about myself the next day. I'd argue with friends and colleagues and be filled with regret, what we now call 'hangxiety'. I'd text lovers and exes when I knew I shouldn't and ruin things between us. Drink had made me cry on paradise beaches around the world.

From the moment my mother had been diagnosed with dementia in the nineties, I'd found relief in the chilled wine in the fridge. Now, my drinking had morphed from a few glasses every night into regular binge-drinking. I reconciled it with myself as something better than before. I wasn't drinking every night, after all – I'd leave two or three days in between. This was much better, I reasoned – it gave the alcohol a chance to leave my body.

At the start of my therapy sessions, I discovered a tiny bar in London and I am sworn to secrecy by its clientele. I sometimes wonder if it ever existed because it seemed to appear in my life when I needed it the most, like a Ghost of Drinking Past.

One day, after a hair appointment in central London, I was starting my long walk home along the canal when I thought I would treat myself to a glass of champagne. I found this largely hidden bar and sat at it by myself, savouring my champagne and wondering why no one else had discovered this little gem.

After about twenty minutes, three silent figures emerged one by one and sat next to me on the bar stools. I thought one of them was meeting someone else because she placed her bag on the stool next to me. No, she was here alone, she told me later. She was a senior healthcare manager and mother of teenagers who just wanted some time to herself. Another was an older lady with a walking stick – she had multiple sclerosis. She said hello to the first lady; obviously they knew each other from previous visits.

The third was a man in his seventies, grey hair slicked back and a paisley cravat adorning his jacket pocket. The ladies nodded as he approached and took his place. They were all obviously regulars.

*There are rules*, they said, as they cautiously brought me into their conversation. *Please don't tell anyone about this place or about us. We want to be able to come here and be anonymous. We don't buy each other drinks. We don't ask each other about our lives. We just come here to drink our champagne. It's cheap here and it's good quality. We usually have three glasses and then go.*

I felt honoured to be welcomed into the group so quickly. They each had a story, which I'm not going to recount here, but they made me realise that histories of hurt can lead to a need to numb our brains with alcohol. We tried to tell ourselves that we were 'just having a nice glass of champagne', but we were pulled together by our shared unhappiness.

I told my therapist about the gathering at the next session. She said it was a beautiful thing that this group of people had been drawn together, yes by their desire for alcohol, but to share their histories of pain. It was another tribe of sorts, and I felt supported by this tiny anonymous group. I went back three or four times between that first visit and Christmas.

My therapist still refused to comment on my drinking as a problem. She always acknowledged what I was saying but she didn't dwell on it or judge me – I was doing that enough for myself. She knew that the root of it all was something so much bigger. In reality, drinking wasn't something I did because I enjoyed it, I did it because I couldn't face the world without it.

My therapist dug and dug away at my childhood pain,

at the loss of my dad at ten. In one session we were discussing the issue of me being 'scary' to men. I had always wondered why men didn't approach me and I always had to do all of the work. I could count the number of times I'd been asked out on one hand – less than one hand – and I hadn't had a boyfriend at all until my late twenties. What was it about me that pushed men away?

My therapist posited a theory that I had constructed a protective fortress around myself after my father died and I was fiercely defending it. Then, leaning forward, she delivered the killer blow. "Lisa, I think there is a bereft orphan inside you."

*A bereft orphan.*

I felt like all the air had been pushed out of my lungs. The words clanged round in my head and in my chest. The moment she uttered the words I could instantly see myself, the girl I had been at ten. There was a picture of her in an album I had at home, taken at school around that time, with a shy smile and yellow panda bobbles in her hair. I now realised that there was hurt in her eyes too. I couldn't wait to get home to search out the photograph and look at her face again.

"Have you ever introduced her to anyone? This Little Lisa?" the therapist asked.

"No... never..." I answered quietly. I was finding it difficult to speak because my brain was overworking, trying to make sense of her words.

*A bereft orphan.*

I had never been introduced to Little Lisa but I'd been protecting her all this time. Here she was, so close I could stroke her hair. She manifested just outside my range of vision, like being able to see a star in the sky more clearly when you don't directly look at it. Here she was, the girl in the picture with her arms wrapped around me, hugging me tightly, her face buried in her arms. I could feel her there – she was with me.

*Hello, Little Lisa.*

"It's alright, you're with me now," I said out loud, smiling, putting the picture of her up on my bookcase before I went to bed. In my mind that night I hugged Little Lisa back, stroked her long, chestnut hair as my mother had once done, and held her tight. I felt so happy to have her at long last.

I felt Little Lisa's presence for weeks and even months after. I took her to work with me and she walked with her hand in mine through Holland Park and laughed at the dogs playing. Slowly, as the days passed, her tight grip around my waist loosened and she simply stayed close to me, by my side all day. I could sense her becoming happier and happier, running ahead of me in the park, and then returning to my side, sometimes for another hug round my middle. It was so real and so vivid. It honestly felt like she was there.

In our next session, I showed the therapist the picture. "Oh there she is," she said in a kindly voice. "How lovely to meet her. Little Lisa."

I couldn't stop grinning. Yes, she was here and she lived with me.

"Do you think she has anything to do with me not wanting children?" I asked.

The therapist paused for a moment. "I can't say with certainty, but it's likely to have something to do with it."

I felt sure that it did. I didn't want children from an early age because I'd already got one – me. And now she was here and I was adopting her. It made me feel indescribably content. All this time, there had been a silent ten-year-old girl inside me who was waiting for her moment, waiting to reclaim the childhood she'd never had. While I'd been looking after her, I hadn't let anyone in, afraid that she would experience more hurt, but now she was ready to play in the sun.

---

I wasn't alone in Agonda that Christmas. Little Lisa returned with me. I would have a family Christmas after all! I wanted to show her the beach and the doughnut dogs and the wild surf – I knew she would love them and I knew I would love having her with me. It wouldn't matter that Shubham wasn't there. I had learned to swim back in the UK and I wanted to plunge into the ocean with Little Lisa and laugh in the crashing waves.

I moved my new family into a hut further back from the beach this time, keen not to be kept awake by said crashing waves and the sounds of Christmas in the restaurant. I couldn't avoid the crows but I was getting used to the ever-present cawing.

Lucia the yoga teacher had decided not to return to Simrose that year, so I was forced to look for classes elsewhere. I already knew that Sampoorna – a local yoga teacher-training school – was running drop-in classes down the road and that they had a really good reputation. I would go there instead, taking Little Lisa with me, of course.

Every morning before 7am, I'd pull my yoga gear on and head through the Simrose restaurant onto the beach. Sweetpea would be waiting below one of the tables, probably having slept there overnight, and she would greet me with her own 'downward dog' pose and produce a morning yowl.

Down on the beach, her three friends from the Jardim resort next door waited on the sand: Sanjo, a large brown and white mongrel, and a brother and sister pair of golden dogs with very short legs, Sherry and Zimbo. This was my pack. I would make a fuss of each one before walking down to the north end of the beach to the river mouth. Captain Nitesh was always there, preparing his boat for the day's trips. He was a friend I'd made on my first visit – he'd taken me to see the dolphins offshore. He'd spot me approaching and raise his hand in a wave, sporting his signature white captain's hat.

Fishermen would be dragging that morning's catch of silvery fish up onto the sand, accompanied by hordes of sea eagles and crows. Beach dogs sat sentinel around them, watching the action as the catch was divided, occasionally barking at other dogs, digging for crabs and rolling around in playfights with each other.

Somewhere behind them I'd hear a chorus of screeching from the trees. When I went to investigate, I found a tree full of fruit bats, stretching their wings out in the sun. I'd seen them flying overhead each evening after sundown, like air-force squadrons in formation. I asked Nitesh where they were going. "A bat party," he said glibly.

Little Lisa loved Agonda as much as I did, perhaps even more. I could feel her joy. After we'd said good morning to the entire beach, we walked back to Simrose where my morning coffee would be ready for me in a small cafetiere. Only then would I be ready to walk down the street to Sampoorna.

The walk to yoga school each morning took me from Simrose to the other end of Agonda's main street, passing Kopi Desa. I knew that if Shubham had been around I wouldn't be making it to the 8.30am class every day because

I'd have been drinking and staying up late. Every cloud had a silver lining. I said *namaste* to Shushant who was always early behind the bar and waved to Charlie, who sold clay cups of chai and omelette sandwiches to passing trade from his little blue cart. I passed Gita setting up her shop and would buy some more sparkly dresses for myself on the way back from class. *Little Lisa loves shiny things*, I thought.

Sampoorna was set off the road, past the colourful Mandala café. Its warm-brown logo was painted on a white wall, with a coloured chalk board listing the drop-in classes. After a short walk up a red dirt road, the Sampoorna 'yoga village' opened out – a muslin-curtained shala in the centre, backed by a restaurant with jewel-coloured cushions on the floor. The jungle rose up at the back of another raised shala, and the whole village was garlanded by tended gardens and brightly coloured huts, where the students stayed.

I came to class every day of my three-week Christmas stay, barring a couple of days where I felt under the weather (I forgot that it's not a good idea to use the tap water to brush your teeth.) I practised ashtanga, vinyasa and yin yoga, and was pleased to discover that the yoga I'd done at home by webcam had prepared me well for real-life classes.

One of the most amazing discoveries I made about yoga (apart from realising that I'd been inadvertently practising it in every contemporary dance class I'd ever done without knowing it) was how much upper body strength it gave me. For the last decade I'd done lower body-based cardio – running and hiking – but here was yoga to give me strength in my arms and shoulders. I felt tall and confident and strong, standing next to happy Little Lisa.

I loved my new routine, with its animals, beach walks, coffee and yoga, but one thing was missing: White Horse. She was nowhere to be seen this time. I asked around and got different answers: "Her owner moved away...", "She's still here..." and the more probable one: "She died..."

My spirit animal was no longer. Was that because she'd already played her role in my life? In Agonda, everything feels like a sign. The universe speaks to you directly in its white light. White Horse had done her job well. Her spirit had ensured that I remained untethered to a man, and she had shown me a life where it was possible to be on your own all day every day, walking up and down a beach, mane blowing in the wind. Who would be my next spirit animal, I wondered? Definitely not Sweetpea. She would just curl up at my feet during breakfast and sigh deeply every ten minutes.

And then I met Alexandra, a Sampoorna yoga teacher. "I recognise you by your hands," she said one day after class.

I held them out. "Yeah, I've got weird fingers," I laughed.

The third fingers on both my hands are not only fore-shortened, they don't have a knuckle either. I'm also in possession of a birthmark on my left little finger that is routinely mistaken for chocolate. As I'm left-handed too, I often joke that I would have been burned at the stake for being a witch had I lived in an earlier century...

But Alexandra said my hands were beautiful. I found her enormously inspiring. Tall and athletic but not skinny, with long, flowing wavy hair, Alexandra commanded each class with her presence. She made it all so accessible – she said yoga wasn't about whether or not we could touch our toes or get our heels on the ground in downward dog – it was about our awareness and our journey there; how we listened to our bodies and celebrated what they could do rather than what they couldn't do. She made us smile with her gentle humour: she told us not to mind the sound of

the crows or the chattering cleaning ladies while we practised – they were just telling each other their stories. I
loved that – everyone was telling their stories in Agonda,
even crows.

I made sure I was in class every time Alexandra was
teaching. I hoped I wasn't coming across like some sort of
groupie as I hung around to chat to her at the end. I just
found her so madly inspiring and I needed that in my life.
Yoga became everything on that holiday, and I wanted to be
clear-headed to do it each morning.

In the evenings, I was mostly avoiding cocktails, and on
the odd occasion that I couldn't resist a sundowner, I
regretted it almost as soon as I'd taken the first sip. Drinking
didn't seem to have the same appeal it once had, or the same
effect. I knew it was all about that first sip for me, and the
anticipation of it. If I got past that stage without giving in, I
was clear. Lime and soda would see me through. The boys
at Kopi started anticipating my choice and I'd leave the bar
early. I knew if Shubham was there I would have carried on
drinking alcohol – perhaps the universe had intervened.

I read an article online about a woman who'd given up
drinking and she described alcohol as a *'toxic depressant'*.
Her piece went on to explain that alcohol is literally poiso-
nous to the body and a hangover is the body's way of trying
to eradicate it. It had the effect of depressing your nervous
system and releasing stimulants that made you anxious and
depressed the next day. Then it would pretend to be the
solution to the problem it had created, and you'd start
drinking again.

*'Toxic depressant'*. Like *'bereft orphan'* the words
clanged in my head, to the point where I was walking
towards Kopi each evening laughing to myself, imagining
ordering "a glass of your best toxic depressant, please!" I

was reducing my intake – not completely, but I was becoming increasingly mindful of alcohol's effects on me.

I thought back to how many arguments I'd had in pubs, how many random men I'd picked up and how many times I'd been unable to get out of bed on a Sunday. I didn't want to be that woman anymore. Even so, I spent the last evening of that holiday in Kopi, getting wasted on sparkling wine again. I'd met a couple who were out drinking and I couldn't sit with them and just drink Diet Coke. I gave in and went for it. It was the last day of my holiday, after all. No matter that I was due to get a taxi to the airport in a few hours.

For a second time, I left Simrose an emotional drunken wreck, late for my taxi and unable to go and say a proper goodbye to Dinesh, or any of the staff at Simrose that I'd come to call my family. Instead, I turned up at the airport and got annoyed about having to wait in a queue. There was a young girl in the seat next to me on the aircraft – I'm pretty sure she cringed when she saw me stumbling towards her, but happily for her, I fell asleep straight away. When I got back from Goa this second time, two things were on my mind: finding a yoga studio and dealing with my drinking.

I'd met four women from West London in Sampoorna who told me about a yoga studio I'd never even heard of – Sangyé – in Kensal Rise. It was literally down the road from me. I tried it out – they practised Jivamukti, which I'd also never heard of, but it had lots of familiar elements from my ashtanga practice. I booked twenty classes for £40. It was a cosy studio and the owner had two dachshunds that ran into class sometimes when we were seated in silence. It was perfect for me.

I also got back to my hiking the day after I landed back in London, and sat next to a woman a few years younger than me on the train. Almost the first topic we got onto was how we were both trying to cut down on our drinking. She recommended I read *This Naked Mind* by Annie Grace and I downloaded the audiobook as soon as I got home.

Annie told me that alcohol was a poison (ethanol) that was made drinkable by the addition of flavourings. It was a toxin that would be banned now if it was introduced as a new foodstuff. She told me that it took ten days to fully leave my system, which meant that for twenty-seven years of my life, alcohol had never left my body. Annie also explained that my feelings about that first drink, the antici-pation of it, was linked to the highly addictive nature of the drug. I wasn't looking forward to a drink because I liked it, I was looking forward to it because my craving would be satisfied.

This was something drinking alcohol had given me – a cycle of craving and reward that just kept getting stronger and stronger over time. Even lengthening the days between binges only had the effect of giving me a bigger reward at the end. I now know that both daily drinking and bingeing are just as bad as each other. There are no benefits to 'days off'. It was all about that first drink, that first sip for me. It was the one that satisfied the craving and everything after that was just back-up.

I was absolutely horrified that I had been doing this for over half of my life. Why had I even started?! I'd managed to avoid smoking, despite everyone around me doing so for years and years. I had congratulated myself on avoiding one carcinogenic drug whilst simultaneously adopting an equally harmful one. Another book – William Porter's *Alcohol Explained* – told me that the UK government made millions of pounds from the alcohol industry (£6.5bn to be exact) – even net of the cost of managing all the alcohol-related problems in the population (£3.5bn) – so they kept quiet about its effects.

I stopped drinking immediately and knew I couldn't go back to it. Ever. I was almost annoyed that *This Naked Mind* stopped me drinking completely – it should have come with a warning on the cover! I felt as though I hadn't had a farewell moment to drink, although that last night in Goa had effectively been it. My final drink was downed on that last night in India: January 10, 2019.

Those first few weeks brought on the 'pink cloud' I'd read about – a feeling of euphoria due to my newly discovered freedom from addiction. I'd also read that it didn't last so I made the most of it. I met friends for drinks but stuck to my lime and soda. There would be a brief moment of longing as I approached the pub but I felt so good knowing I wouldn't be the one asking if anyone else wanted 'just one more' or trying to arrange some sort of afterparty on a Tuesday night.

During those early weeks, I experienced moments of FAB – Fading Affect Bias – where my brain remembered the best bits of drinking rather than the awful ones. So I made a list of everything I wasn't proud of doing while drunk and read it every time I felt like the nostalgia was creeping back in. As Annie Grace and William Porter said, the good times I had were because I was with friends enjoying a day or night out, not because of the toxic depressant I was drinking. It had lied and convinced me that it was responsible for it all.

My friends reacted very supportively to my news, some of them deciding on the spot to give up themselves. I'd read somewhere that people are just looking for permission to give up and it looked as though that was true. Drinking is something that relies on groupthink – it requires everyone to opt in and those who opt out to be viewed as suspicious. If I'd tried to give up in the ladette nineties, I would never have been able to do it, but the timing at that point – alongside the burgeoning wellness trend – made it all the more possible. Alcohol-free drinks were becoming more mainstream and people were less likely to think I was weird for opting out, especially if they were millennials or younger. I found the younger members of my publishing team completely inspiring in that respect. They told me that alcohol was too expensive and that they had better things to spend their money on.

After my first month of sobriety, I realised that the emergence of Little Lisa had given me such a sense of deep contentment. She was my little girl and I loved her. Now I had her with me, there was no need to numb the pain of existence with alcohol. I simply didn't feel like I needed it anymore. I could see that other people were masking pain with alcohol and it made me more empathetic. Every time I saw a drunk on the street in London, I wondered what pain he or she had suffered to get them to that stage of their addiction. And it was an addiction. Those people were not different from me or any other drinkers – just further down an inevitable road. It's not that they 'couldn't handle it', as society had us believe. We were all potential alcoholics because we were dealing with a highly addictive drug.

---

Back in September 2018, I'd been on a trekking holiday to Kyrgyzstan with my hiking group and had to return to the guest house in the middle of day one because of intense hip pain. All we'd done was walk round a market in the capital,

Bishkek. I cried and wanted to go home, but my hiking tribe rallied round. I decided to keep going – one day at a time.

On the first day of hiking, I was descending a very steep mountain pass and cried again. I was in agony. I knew I couldn't continue – I would hold the group up. I ran through the get-out options in my head but they were limited – we were hundreds of miles into a no man's land between the Kyrgyz border and the Tien Shan mountains that border China. We were trekking with nomads and their horses were carrying our tents and food. The hike leader, Gary, saw me crying and asked me if I wanted to get on a horse.

"I'm fine!" I replied.

Gary turned to me and said, matter-of-factly, "You can hike anywhere, but when can you go horseriding with nomads?"

But still I refused. I would grin and bear the pain. There was a rule amongst hikers that you shouldn't complain about anything. Everyone had something they could complain about, like blisters or knee pain, but they kept quiet.

After lunch was over, I was removing my boots to cross a shallow river when I saw one of the horsemen beckoning me over. He was called Tashtemir, meaning 'son of iron', and he sported a blue-velvet tabard over trousers tucked into boots, a black astrakhan hat and sunglasses. He was smoking a roll-up. He gestured for me to mount the horse that he was leading behind him. I gave in. The pain in my hip was too much. I had to be pushed up on to the horse by some of the other horsemen.

As soon as we began slowly clip-clopping across the shallow stream in the remote valley, the biggest grin spread across my face. The pain in my hip ebbed and I was suddenly aware of where I was and what I was doing. I felt euphoric.

"Tchoo! Tchoo!" Tashtemir cried at the horses, to make them go faster. As we rode between the snow-capped mountains, he began calling out names of animals he could see in the valleys to either side of us. "Yak! Ibex!" We would eat both of them in stews later.

I felt incredibly happy as I helped the horsemen pitch the tents, then watched them ride off to fetch the other hikers before the sun went down. There was a cloud of dust around them as they galloped away. It reminded me of *The Magnificent Seven*.

On my return to the UK, I told my therapist about what had happened with Tashtemir and her conclusion was simple: "You let others help and support you," she said. "Not everything in life has to be a punishing solo challenge. You have nothing to prove."

I realised how much I'd punished myself over the years – like a good Catholic girl – for no other reason than to prove I could handle it. I'd punished myself through exercise and diet, through work, and I had done it with alcohol and throwing myself at the wrong men. I was starting to ask myself why I'd done those things, and what other choices I could have made.

I'd also been in regular physiotherapy sessions for months to combat recurring hip and shoulder pain. Both my physio- and my psychotherapist concurred – many of my problems were caused by stress. I didn't believe them at first. I thought I was just getting old. After all, I was over fifty.

In yoga class, Alexandra had told us that our hips store stress and emotion. She'd asked us if we'd ever burst into tears in 'pigeon pose'. I had! The pose involved lying prone on the floor, with one knee drawn forward towards the chest. In class after a particularly stressful event at work, I'd begun to cry in this pose and I thought I'd simply been overwhelmed by what had happened. Alexandra said that our hips and chest tighten when we experience trauma and we subconsciously curl into the foetal position to protect ourselves. We can become very emotional when we uncurl.

I had dealt with continuous hip and shoulder pain over the past few years and now I knew the reason why. It wasn't just being hunched over a desk or my phone all day, although those things didn't help. It all suddenly made sense.

I had been a senior manager in publishing for twenty-three years, and I had been dealing with some of the most toxic people you could ever work with for the last decade. They were people who didn't like my honest approach, and fundamentally they were people who enjoyed pulling others down so they could get ahead. The women were even worse than the men.

I had been the defensive wall in front of my teams for too long and my therapist said it was time for "mum to step down and let her grown-up children fight their own battles." Thus far, I'd taken all the hits thrown their way. For a creative industry, publishing had a very strange view of its creative teams. It appeared to value numbers-people in the business more, even though there would be no numbers to crunch without the products made by creatives. In editorial, I'd fought a constant battle with sales and finance people who thought we just corrected spelling. They didn't seem to realise (or want to acknowledge) that we were the ones with the publishing ideas.

I'd also hit a 'wooden ceiling', where, as a woman of a certain age without an Oxbridge education, my time in corporate publishing was borrowed. I hadn't networked as I should have done because I honestly didn't know it was a thing until it was too late. I didn't know I was supposed to shore up my career by having secret coffees or cocktails with top people. I'm not even sure that strategy would have worked anyway – I was from the north-west and went to a Catholic comprehensive school and a non-redbrick university. I'd done well to get as far as I had in an industry largely based on an old school-tie network.

By early 2019, on my return from Goa, I was done. Even though I loved my team and the books we published, it was time to move on. I'd freelance while I decided what I was going to do and write the book I'd always wanted to write.

It was momentous for me. Up until then, I had always defined myself by my job. My teams had almost become family to me and I felt maternal towards them, especially the young ones. I loved steering them through difficult creative challenges. Creative people are often open and emotional, and I loved that about them. The problem was that I was emotional too, and managing people brought a lot of emotional strain with it, especially while fending off attacks from departments who didn't understand what we were doing.

In the spring, it was time to move on: from the UK, from the corporate world, and most importantly, from my former drinking, self-punishing self. I decided to move on from men (Shubham would clearly now be on an eternal cruise ship), so I rented out my flat, put my stuff in storage and decided not to go back to Agonda. Pastures new beckoned.

"But why have you decided not to go back there?" my therapist asked in our last-ever session. "This is a place that you call home, with people you call family, and animals you love. This is a place where you have found peace and contentment, where you have taken Little Lisa. Isn't this the home you can return to again and again?"

She was right. In Agonda, I'd discovered a more peaceful, authentic version of myself; one that valued walking on the beach, saying hello to stray dogs and strangers, with sea-salted hair and no makeup. People smiled and said hello to me. The defensive forcefield I'd carried around since I was ten was slowly coming down. Yoga was the practice that helped force open the locks along with the therapy, but Agonda was responsible for calming my mind and spirit. And then I found out that Shubham was back home.

On my first day back in Agonda in March 2019, I went to afternoon yoga at Sampoorna. Afterwards, I bought a hot chai from Charlie and waved at Gita who was wearing her new glasses. "You're back already?!" she shouted.

"Can't stay away!" I answered, grinning.

And there he was, Shubham, looking down, frowning at a drink he was mixing. He looked up and grinned. "And what...?"

And what ... was drinking a blueberry and pineapple juice smoothie he blended for me.

And what ... was arranging to come back to see him that night and selecting a dress I knew he'd like.

And what ... was getting on the back of his new Royal Enfield bike at the end of the night and whizzing towards Simrose, as I'd last done very early on New Year's Day over a year ago and longed to do ever since.

However, I had come to Goa with a plan and it wasn't going to be directed by a man. I would do early morning yoga and write this book. Although it was almost like a dream to see Shubham again, I worried about how his presence might impact everything else I wanted to do, so I had rules I was ready to put in place.

The next morning, before I could utter a word, Shubham leapt out of bed, exclaiming, "You must do your yoga and write your book!" and promptly jumped on his Enfield to head home.

I was utterly amazed. Most men I'd known hadn't given a toss about supporting my ambitions. And not even 'most men' – all of the men. But every day after that, Shubham asked me how my yoga practice had gone and how many words I'd written, while he made me a mocktail. Unicorn Man.

I had one difficult week when I was writing the first section of this book and retreading old ground – times in my life where I had felt deeply unhappy. The writing was dredging up feelings I hadn't expected to encounter again. I got to Kopi that night, and not knowing what was in my head, Shubham immediately told me that he and the boys had a plan to take me to Ozrem for the day – a nearby river where they often went for beers and a barbecue. How perfect! It was just what I needed to hear. "When are we going?" I asked. Shubham couldn't quite say – deciding on an actual day seemed to be a task for another time – but I was happy that there was even a plan in the first place.

I'd been so sick of making my own fun for so many years. Every birthday, every holiday, every weekend away – I'd had to arrange it all. And any 'spoiling rotten' had, of course, all fallen to me. I longed for someone else to arrange something for me – no matter how small. A picnic, a drive, a night in a hotel – something, anything.

The next day, while we waited for the actual date for

Ozrem to be confirmed, Shubham took me to nearby Cabo de Rama on his bike. I'd been before, to the old Portuguese fort that overhangs the sea, but I wanted to explore Shubham's home turf with him.

After yoga, breakfast and a bit of writing ("You must write your book first!"), he picked me up at Simrose and we sped off on his Enfield. I was scared, even though I knew he'd been riding one of these since he was in the womb – but it wasn't him I was worried about. It was the other bikes, tuktuks, lorries, cows and dogs that worried me.

Riding or driving through India is like being in a videogame where obstructions are thrown at you unexpectedly. We had a few near misses, but Shubham just laughed them off. He also laughed as I dug my fingers into him every time we banked round a corner, but he slowed down so I wouldn't be too scared. "Don't worry!" he'd shout occasionally, but it would take more than his reassuring words to do that. I sang the Gayatri mantra behind him, to take my mind off the road.

Every time I got on Shubham's bike I gripped a little less ferociously, and laughed at myself wearing his *Great Escape*-style green helmet. None of the locals wore anything on their heads unless the police were doing checks, and even then, they signalled to one another as a warning and wore a helmet just to go through the checkpoint. I loved that we rode for a while on an unfinished dual carriageway. Everyone was using it and going the wrong way. Cows, dogs, people out for a Sunday stroll – everyone was out for a walk in all directions. It was peak India.

After visiting the fort, we rode to the Cabo de Rama beach nearby. We pulled up to the vast bush 'car park' on top of the cliffs and headed down the rough path that was cut into the red stone. There was nothing there except a lifeguard under a palm-frond shelter, and a gang of young local boys messing about in the water. They stared at me, with my white skin in a pink bikini. Shubham told them to move away, then held my hand as we waded into the big waves.

I'd only learnt to swim in the few months before that trip and had never swum in the sea until that Christmas, where I'd only managed four backstrokes before panicking in the strong waves. Now my hand was being held as we walked into the waves past the point where they broke. Beyond that, all was calm, and I could stand up in the water.

"Don't be scared," said Shubham. "You are scared of everything."

When we finally got to Ozrem with Ram and Shubham 2 the following week, I was even scared of getting into the river. We'd had a longer bike ride to get there and my legs were wobbling from the experience. I perched on a rock to recover, watching the boys build a barbecue out of found materials – rocks and a bit of mesh – and marvelled at their mackerel-gutting skills. They cracked open beers for themselves and supplied 0% Bavaria lager for me. Ram pronounced it 'Bavariya', rhyming with Maria.

Once Shubham had completed his barbecue duties he beckoned to me, holding his hand out. "Let's go for a shower," he said, meaning a swim in the river.

He led me in slowly over the slippery stones and held both my hands as I found my feet. He then swam a few feet away and asked me to swim to him for practice. Small fish were flitting around my legs and occasionally nibbling the backs of my legs.

"It's just feesh," Shubham said, as I squealed in fear.

While I practised breaststroke in the shallows,

Shubham dived into the water and reappeared standing on a small stone bank in the middle of the river. He looked beautiful in the water. His oiled black hair turned a silvery grey and his droplet-covered face lit up in the sunshine. He was holding a drowned dragonfly aloft on his palm. "It might come back to life!" he said, watching it carefully as it dried out in the sun. I took mental pictures of the image because I wasn't sure if I'd see him again once he was back on his next cruise ship.

Shubham was smiling and laughing: "I am jolly," he said.

*This is how it's supposed to be*, I thought. *This is how it's supposed to be when a man is truly with you, when he's not scared of you and doesn't resent you in any way. He wants to show you the places that make him happy and wants you to be unafraid. He wants you to practice yoga and write your book. He wants to take lots of pictures of you on the beach. He wants to save dragonflies from drowning. He wants you to feel free.*

On the bike on the way back home, the red sun setting over the hills behind Agonda, I felt a happiness I hadn't ever felt before and I gave him an extra squeeze around his middle.

"And what...?"

There is something about Agonda that attracts strong, independent women. On my second visit, I'd noticed women my age and older, stalking down the beach with their deep tans, silver hair and yoga bodies. I wanted to be them, especially when I saw them sitting in Agonda's coffee shops, sipping masala chai, chatting with equally Amazonian friends. I'd also been hugely inspired by Alexandra, whom I was convinced was from Wonder Woman Island.

I started to notice women of all ages on their own, walking up and down the beach or whizzing past me on bikes. They weren't wearing makeup, sometimes clad in only a bikini, hair screwed up into a top knot or wrapped in a scarf, just walking or riding with their thoughts. When I'm on holiday, it takes me days to stop wearing makeup, to stop worrying about what my hair looks like or agonising over what I'm going to wear. I looked at these women and wanted to be part of their tribe – the 'women with zero fucks'.

Back in London, my feminist friends and I *said* that we gave zero fucks, but most of us did – spending all our time and money on getting our roots done, buying expensive clothes and makeup we didn't need, dieting obsessively and thrashing ourselves in the gym. And on top of all that, we did those things whilst trying to hold down big 'important' jobs. And yet here was this alternative way of life, an 'island' of women doing exactly the opposite, looking happier than anyone I'd ever come across. Women feel safe in Goa. It's one of the safest regions in India for women, and the evidence was all around me. Here we all were, all the single ladies, having a lovely time. With ourselves.

In my first week back at Simrose, I met Juliet, a British woman in her sixties who rented a small pink cottage on the beach. I hadn't noticed the cottage before, but there it was, nestling between two resorts, like an icing-sugar house. It was like something out of a fairy tale. Juliet was a Buddhist who lived in the north of India running a stray-dog clinic. She came to Agonda every year for a couple of months, just before monsoon when it was quiet. She came to Simrose to drink masala chai and write her book on her iPad. Writing books seemed to be the thing all the solo women were doing out there – we were all telling our stories.

Juliet told me about a part of the beach at the other end of Agonda, where we could swim in a wave-free part of the ocean. We started meeting down there every afternoon and spread our towels and sarongs out on the hot flat rocks at the back of the beach. We waded into the water, followed by the pack of dogs that cooled their paws there. I practised my swimming strokes in the gentler waters and Juliet told me about her life in the north with her dogs and the Buddhist monks.

I'd only ever been to Goa and I longed to see other parts of India. Juliet told me that where she lived in Bodh Gaya, all life – and death – was out there on the streets. Years before, she had found herself on the steps of a Buddhist temple, led there after a life of self-harm through drugs and drink. There, she found peace. She had devoted her life ever since to looking after the monks and the temple dogs and her eyes sparkled with light.

Juliet had long white hair and I asked her if she'd ever coloured it. She was a henna devotee, she said, but when she decided to ditch it at a certain age, her eighty-year-old mother had been horrified. She was still colouring her hair and couldn't understand why her daughter wouldn't while she was still 'young'. I told her I thought it looked magnificent.

I'd been colouring my hair for years and had been toying with the idea of just letting the grey grow through. No one bothered about things like that in Agonda. I'd stopped wearing any makeup in India apart from mascara – anything like foundation or tinted moisturiser turned green in the bright light. Hair colour looked fake in the strong sun.

When I mentioned my hair to Gita, she looked at me

quizzically. "Why do you want to colour your hair? Just leave it." Of course, she had a full head of shiny long black hair oiled back into a bun.

When I asked Shubham if he'd still like me with silver hair, he said, "Just be natural."

I'd worried about my root growth on previous visits and had timed hair appointments around my flights. This was the first time I'd just let it all go and it felt so good. But I feared it wouldn't feel as good back in London, with a badger stripe along my parting. So I booked a hair appointment for my first weekend back and would see how I felt then. My red hair defined me; I was Redwoods, after all.

As the sun went down on our swimming beach each evening, Juliet and I would hug each other, congratulating ourselves on not needing a cocktail to witness it. We'd both given up alcohol and that made us very unusual among the British tourists in Goa. I recalled wanting to do a beach pub crawl on my second visit – but it had never happened, thankfully. Agonda just wasn't that place. It was a place for yoga and walking on the beach early in the morning with the dogs, watching the morning catch come in on the fishing boats. Hangovers just spoiled it.

It was during that trip that I switched from enjoying sunsets to sunrises. I realised that I'd been equating sunset with a time to start drinking and then missing the most hope-filled, sparkling-bright time of day: the morning. Why celebrate the sun going down when you could see it coming up? I reasoned.

Juliet and I had both made friends with 'Turtle Guy' – the man who slept in a shelter on the beach next to the turtle 'nursery'. It was just outside Juliet's pink cottage. Agonda is an official Olive Ridley turtle nesting site and Turtle Guy was there to make sure the babies made it into the ocean. They are a threatened species. Outside his shelter, there was a fenced-off area containing a netted grid. When the eggs were laid, he and another official would transfer them to the nursery for safety. They didn't want dogs digging them up, or tourists trying to take them home. Turtle Guy told us about one German woman who'd popped one in her bag when he wasn't looking.

The eggs would take forty-five to fifty days to hatch, and Turtle Guy would then transfer them to his shelter, into a bowl filled with seawater. Juliet and I watched the tiny babies in the first batch, only a couple of inches long, click-clacking around as they scrambled to leave the bowl.

Turtle Guy waited until darkness fell to release them, to give them the best chance of survival. The odds seemed insurmountable to me – those huge crashing waves versus those tiny creatures. I'd been told that their mothers knew when they were hatching and waited offshore for their babies when the time came. Turtle Guy said that was a myth that tourists liked to believe. In reality, those baby turtles were out there completely on their own, striving to survive, with no safety net. That sounded all too familiar.

One night during my second week, Juliet and I went to help Turtle Guy release a new batch of baby turtles but some drunken tourists wandered up with their camera phones. One of the women stepped backwards and accidentally trod on a turtle and killed it. Juliet slapped her legs in anger. "Stupid woman!!"

Turtle Guy was so angry and upset, he scooped all the babies back up again into the bowl before striding back to his shelter with them. We followed him at a distance, saying we would leave him in peace, but he beckoned to us to stay. "We will wait for THEM to go," he said, gesturing towards the tourists. "YOU can stay and help."

After everyone else had gone, we accompanied Turtle Guy back down to the shoreline and he shone a lamp at the water's edge, mimicking the moon. "Put them on the sand, one by one," he instructed. "They will follow the light into the sea."

And we did, between us, laying them carefully on the sand, watching their little flippers pull them towards the waves. In one watery swipe, they were gone.

---

One day, I was at the swimming beach alone and I wasn't really comfortable. I was worried about swimming without Juliet around to save me should the need arise, and this was an area where people, usually local boys, came to party.

Looking behind me, I saw a European woman stretched out on a rock. She was deeply tanned – she'd obviously been in India a long time to get that mahogany colour – and she was wearing a brown bikini and a cap pulled over her face. When she walked into the water next to me, she'd taken the cap off and I could see she had dark grey hair and no makeup. *Here's another one*, I thought. Wonder Woman Island. We nodded at each other and continued in our solitude, just happy to have another woman around.

As the sun started to set, we were both stretched out on the beach drying off, when suddenly the woman was standing over me, blocking out the sun. "Hello, I was going to walk up onto the rocks to watch the sunset. Would you like to join me?" Her accent was German.

"Oh...er..." I delayed my response, knowing that my first instinct would be to say no. I took a millisecond to have a word with myself. I remembered Su-Bo and the sunset bike ride in Thailand. *Always say yes*, Lisa, *always say yes when a woman asks you to watch the sun go down with her.*

So I followed her up onto the nearby rocks, not knowing where she was taking me. I had covered up my bikini body with a voluminous kaftan, but Ida, as she introduced herself, picked her way up the rocks in just her brown bikini and a pair of thick sliders. "Just take your valuables," she'd said, so I'd grabbed my bag full of stuff. Ida had simply brought a cap with her room key inside it.

She took me up onto the rocky promontory south of Agonda beach. I'd looked at it from Simrose on every visit but had never walked to it. I'd only just discovered the swimming beach, after all. As we sat on the highest rock watching the sun go down, the stretch of Agonda beach behind us, Ida told me about her life in India. She was fifty-five and had left a senior-management job in Munich two years previously to come to India. She'd visited ashram after ashram, meditating every day. "Just 'being', not 'doing'," she said.

I told her my story and said that I was fascinated by the number of women who appeared to be doing what she was doing here in Agonda – just existing and not trying to be anything but themselves.

"India does that to you," she said, looking out to sea, stretching out her brown legs. I noticed that she hadn't shaved them.

I could feel India doing the same thing to me and I longed to go feral – let the hairs on my legs and the grey hair on my head grow out. *Oh god*, I thought, *I'm such a cliché.* I told Ida that I'd been thinking about alternative lifestyles, like hers.

"It's all about return on your investment," she said. "You have to work out how much it costs you to hold down a big job, live in a big flat in a big city, and go on big holidays to reward yourself after all the stress. What is the return on your investment? And I don't just mean money. What are you actually getting out of it emotionally, physically or financially?"

I was firmly in the red, in almost every sense. To me, a big job had always been the end game, especially as it allowed me to go on holidays like this one. My sense of self-worth came from being successful in the workplace – from my job title and the size of my team, to winning awards and being recognised as a super-achiever. I'd built a life that revolved around work and recognition, but here, I was starting to think in a new way. What did all that really matter?

Ida had led me up onto the rocks to deliver a sermon that would change my life. Even her name was significant – in Indian philosophy, the Ida is the name given to the left side of the body and the energy channels that flow through it. The Ida is characterised by the feminine, the moon, the mind, coolness and introversion. Agonda was at it again with its massive signs from the universe.

---

Shubham had gone back to work on another cruise ship and I was now a fully paid-up member of Wonder Woman Island. Every day, I headed to Sampoorna Yoga School to join around fifteen women in yoga class, with perhaps one or two men. It was part of my new ritual – like a moment of prayer – arriving in my space on the mat next to the shala curtain and the jungle beyond it. I got to know the teachers and they got to know me, over masala chai outside the shala. They were all young women half my age, but in the yoga world, age is irrelevant. Everyone looked youthful and vibrant. I call it Yoga Face.

One day, when we were having chai on Juliet's pink and white balcony, she asked me why I wasn't doing the yoga teacher training, especially as I was at Sampoorna all the time anyway.

"Me? I'm not good enough," I answered. Something sounded very wrong with that statement, even as I said it.

I'd taught ballet for years in my late teens and early twenties – I wasn't good enough at ballet either, but I'd been a good teacher. I'd meant for it to be my career until I'd had the calling to go to university at the grand old age of twenty-two.

"You could do it," Juliet said. "If I can do it, anyone can!"

She'd trained to teach in Rishikesh, the spiritual home of yoga. Now she just did her own practice, on the balcony outside the little pink house on the beach. "I think you'd be great. Think about it!" she said.

I did think about it and soon it became all I thought about. I spoke to some yogis at Sampoorna about it too. One of the teachers said I had a 'strong practice', which was news to me. All I could see was other people in amazing poses that I hadn't got a hope in hell of achieving. But then I remembered what Alexandra had said at Christmas about the importance of listening to your own body and being grateful for the things it 'could' do.

My head was saying, *"Go back home, regroup, wash your clothes, get your roots done, lie in your own bed and decide what to do next."*

And yet my heart was saying, *"Stay, stay in this place that you love. Stop worrying... Learn to teach – you've done it before. Maybe it's meant to be. Let the universe decide."*

Could I be one of the women I admired on Wonder Woman Island? In the future, could women see my tanned yoga body on the beach, with no makeup and silver hair, and think, "I want to be her..."? Could I live in a little pink cottage on the beach? Could I live in India at all, never mind through monsoon time?

I knew I was in danger of becoming even more of a cliché. I'd asked Gita if she practised yoga and she'd told me it was only for rich, white women. Women like her were too busy working to do yoga. I had been living in a holiday bubble but I knew the reality would be very different. But ultimately, did fantasies like this come true for people like me? Until then, I had lived in a world that had offered me dying parents, stressful jobs and disappointing men. I wasn't used to good things happening to me, only achievements garnered through hard, often punishing, graft.

I didn't know what the future held, but I knew that it didn't need a man to complete the picture. Shubham had showed me what being with a man could be, but he was twenty-six and from a relatively conservative community where I would have to be kept a secret. I had been a man's secret for far too long and I wanted to stand in the daylight and be seen. I wanted to be seen as the authentic me, Amazonian me, here in this matriarchal community by the sea. I wanted to feel physically strong and to help people feel the same way as I did, just as the women in Agonda had done for me.

On the last weekend of my holiday, Easter weekend, I lazed on the swimming beach for one last time with Juliet. A young girl came to the rock that Ida had lain on and spread her sarong out on it. She said hello.

She was called Amondine, from Switzerland, and she'd been travelling solo around the world, ending up in India.

She was in her early twenties and had finally kicked an eating disorder. She felt alive and well here, she said.

"India does that to you," Juliet and I said in unison and laughed.

"I'm here to do yoga teacher training," she announced, brightly.

Juliet looked at me. I knew what she was thinking.

"Ok, ok, I get it. I'm doing this. I'm applying for teacher training at Sampoorna."

Juliet waved her arms around in delight and hugged me.

Goddamn universe.

———

I didn't quite feel like a yoga goddess when I entered Sampoorna as a full-time yoga-teaching student in May 2019. I'd pushed my body hard at the drop-in classes, despite a painful shoulder, and now it was making me think I'd made completely the wrong decision. On the day I should have flown home from Goa at the end of April I ran in a panic into the school, certain that I should be on that plane and not putting my body through another month of intensive training in humid, pre-monsoon Goa. Luckily, I found Danni and Karen – my ashtanga and vinyasa teachers – sitting on the jewel-coloured cushions by the dining area.

"You're here, so just do it. Trust the process," Danni said, in her strong Irish accent, her long, brown, curly hair wrapped up in a scarf. "The fact that you've got an injury will play in your favour. It will give you even greater body awareness and you can modify everything."

But I didn't want to modify anything – I wanted to be my best yoga self.

"That's your ego talking," Karen said, her bright blue eyes shining. "This is not about how brilliant you are at the poses. You will learn to leave your ego at the door here."

So I missed the flight that night, and I am a person who never misses flights. I was unable to change it so I was simply a 'no-show' and it freaked me out. I booked another ticket for the end of that month and lay awake all night thinking about the flight I wasn't on and my empty seat. I would count down every day of the course until it was time to go home to my comfort zone.

There were only three or four of us who weren't young girls in our twenties on the course. In my first week (of four) I met a Yorkshirewoman, Chris, who was in her sixties. We stuck together from that moment on, even though we were in different teaching groups. We marvelled at these shiny new young women who had all their lives before them. I felt broken due to my shoulder and the fact that I'd just written the first draft of this book before the course. Could I get through this?

Chris' attitude was calm and strong. She was a hatha yoga practitioner, a slower, gentler yoga style than the ones we were studying, and she was kind to her body. She encouraged me to be kind to mine. Chris had beautiful white hair and an open smiling face: Yoga Face. It was lovely to see the transformation happen on the younger girls' faces as the weeks went by. My friends noticed my own face changing on my intermittent Facebook posts. "You look so young!" they said.

Chris and I had bonded during a partner-work session where we held the hands of everyone in the group, one by one, and looked into their eyes. I still don't know why that simple gesture elicited so much emotion but it did. I suppose we rarely do it, especially in big cities where the aim is to avoid eye contact at all costs. It's easier to push people away when you haven't looked in their eyes and seen that they are a person with feelings just like you.

When it was her turn with me, Chris stood silently, squeezing my hands and nodding her head, as if to say, *"It's ok, I am here and you are calm."* She didn't cry when almost everyone else did – she was a source of comfort to everyone.

In the second week, we learned about '*ahimsa*' – non-violence – from our philosophy teacher, Sudhir, an ex-Hindu monk. This was one of Sage Patanjali's '*yamas*' – life values – in the 'eight limbs' of yoga he created three thousand years ago. Ahimsa was popularised by Gandhi but I'd never really considered the term properly until then. Ahimsa should be applied to our thoughts, words and actions, Sudhir said, in our dealings with other living beings. We also learned that we could be violent to ourselves and I knew I had been, by bashing my shoulder through endless yoga classes when it was crying out to be left alone to heal.

As the days ticked by, I thought more and more about ahimsa and modified every pose during our daily 6.30am ashtanga practice with Danni, using blocks and a strap. Why had I been trying to do everything my body wasn't ready to do? Who was I trying to impress? My yoga practice was for myself and no one else, so I was simply feeding my own ego by punishing my body. It had to stop.

Sudhir said that poses were only a small part of living a yogic life. They represented only one of the eight limbs of Patanjali's yoga. They were designed to help the mind free itself from the ego and all mental distractions, and prepare it for sitting for long periods in meditation. In the West, we'd turned yoga into a workout and prided ourselves on our ability to do a handstand or an arm balance. "The reason you are getting injured through yoga in the West is because you push your bodies too far before they are ready," Sudhir said.

*Guilty as charged, m'lud.*

I spent a lot of study time (and beach walks) thinking about how much the rest of my life needed a policy change. I thought about ahimsa, and I realised the stress of my recent working life was an act of violence on myself. I'd had to seek physiotherapy to deal with the physical effects of it, and psychotherapy to deal with the emotional ones. The alcohol I needed to numb the pain was an act of violent self-harm on my body, and the processed food I put in it was just as bad. I hadn't even begun on the number of men I'd allowed to hurt me over the years.

I had to acknowledge that I had been harmful to other people too. I'd hurt Graham by marrying him, knowing it was the wrong thing to do, and then by cheating on him to get out of the situation. I had harmed myself and other women by operating in that dark place with married men. I'd argued with friends and colleagues under the influence of alcohol and hurt my own body during binge sessions. The fortress I'd been defending around Little Lisa made my attacks even worse.

Sudhir spoke of our need to punish and reward our bodies in order to 'deserve' what we thought was 'happiness'. "We punish ourselves with exercise and then reward ourselves with food and drink afterwards," he said. "In order to deserve those things, we think we need to take the punishment first. But happiness is our birthright, we don't need to deserve it. It is ours already."

Ours was a very Western, Christian response to the world, I thought. In Western faiths, humans are inherently bad and have to spend their lives atoning for their sins, especially Catholic humans like me. But Sudhir told us that in Indian philosophy, joy was our true nature. We didn't have to work for it; it was simply there. We just needed to access it by stripping away any mental obstructions formed during adult life. We could see that joy in children and dogs who didn't have any worldly worries. Most importantly, we didn't need to strive to be more than we were, we were enough.

*We were loved.* I had heard yoga teachers say that before and I was keen to know by whom. What if you had no loved ones, not even a pet? Who was doing the loving then?

I asked the question at a *satsang* (gathering) one evening, as we all sat around Sudhir, in his signature neatly pressed white shirt and chinos. His small rectangular glasses were perched on the end of his nose and his trademark grin was in place, his silver-black hair cut short. Sitting on his haunches, barefoot atop a plastic chair, Sudhir explained: "Love is the nature of the self. It's in us. It's not coming from somewhere else. When the mind is disturbed, we don't experience that love. But, in the presence of some people, our mental blocks get cleared – we experience that love and we think it's coming from them. A mother experiences that love from a child, parents experience it from their children, partners experience it from each other. But what is happening is that in their presence, the mind and heart are being cleared. The clouds go away and you experience the sun. The sun is always shining and so are love and joy, our true nature. Even if someone has no close family members, they can experience that love in their work, their passions, their friends."

Even before I got to Sampoorna I knew yoga had silently been working its magic on me for over a year, giving me a clearer head, and a happier, calmer demeanour. I knew, because people smiled at me more. I had Yoga Face. Removing alcohol from my life made the effect more stark.

I felt like I'd had a factory reset; it was a return to someone I was before I started drinking – fresher, more youthful, and better able to cope with life. Suddenly everything made more sense. I'd been looking for love and joy all around the world, ever since I'd lost my father. And it was right there inside me all along. I'd already found it in Little Lisa.

I was also, surprisingly, someone more introverted, as I'd been when I first arrived in London from North Wales. The notes I got back on my first teaching session said that my voice couldn't be heard. *What?!* But this was me: the publisher who regularly gave speeches and presentations in front of hundreds of people. My voice was my thing! But here I was too quiet and not forceful enough. I realised that I'd faked a level of extroversion in my working life in order to get ahead, to be Redwoods, but here it had been stripped away. I was humbled by yoga and I almost had to learn to speak again. Telling someone how to move into *adho mukha svanasana* (downward-facing dog pose) was suddenly the hardest thing in the world.

"You have the freedom to choose how you respond to any situation," Sudhir said, "even though you can't affect the outcome. You can choose to be angry or stressed in a bad situation or remain calm and deal with it. You can simply do what needs to be done, and the totality [the universe] will take care of things."

The simplicity of all of this philosophy blew my mind. I would do what needed to be done and find a way to live a different life.

As part of our training, we were offered the chance to have a Silent Day. Initially, fuelled by an apparent lack of study time, the answer from the group was riddled with panicky 'no's. But Chris and I and a few others were thinking, '*I bet this is going to be one of the most profound experiences of the whole thing*' and backed the plan. In the end, most people agreed to go for it.

One of the five '*niyamas*' or personal practices, in Sage Patanjali's eight limbs of yoga is *tapas*. It is the practice of removing yourself from your comfort zone so you can understand and harness your desires. Fasting, silence, giving up your smartphone – these are all part of the same practice.

"You will not be allowed to speak to each other," Sudhir said, "or even look at each other. You cannot read anything, listen to music or look at your phones. The wifi will be switched off. The only thing you are allowed to do is journal the experience. You are free to absorb the nature around you and reflect internally on yourself."

I was excited at the prospect. I was intrigued to see where my mind would take me. It was already pretty active so what would it do if it was given a whole day to run riot? I would write it all down in the little peacock-print beaded notebook in which I had notes for this book and all my study notes from the course.

---

*The day begins with a mysore practice of ashtanga – silent and self-conducted – but we are all together in the same shala, which is conveniently outside my room. It has a view out over the roof of the house next door to Sampoorna and I like to watch the owner's scraggy dog find a place on the roof* and have a lie down every morning. A cock crows on the wall, strutting around, being followed by his lady friend.

My shoulder is extremely painful so I modify every move. I need to be kinder to my shoulder – to my body, I think. It can do so much, so beautifully. It can dance, hike and practice yoga and I am grateful to it.

After ninety minutes of practice, I get to savasana – corpse pose – and I cry silent tears. I have had a sudden overwhelming joyous memory of being at university in a contemporary dance class with my friends. I felt the joy of moving in a group as one unit then, and I feel it return in this shala. Chris is lying next to me, of course. She is never far from me. Perhaps I don't like being alone in the world as much as I think.

Whilst lying there, hearing my fellow yogis breathing and completing their last asanas, I think of the swimming beach and how Juliet encouraged me over and over to come to Sampoorna. I think of baptism and rebirth, and think 'this is the place I have done it.' I have been born again. I am the person I was when I was a young woman. She is back. Little Lisa.

I sit next to Chris at silent breakfast and I am dying to share my thoughts, but I stare at my plate instead. I realise that I seek validation from eye contact with people and if they withhold it I panic about not being liked. I know my defensive wall around Little Lisa has led me to be a bit spiky and scary and I worry that I've pushed people away. Do what needs to be done. Stop defending something that doesn't require it anymore.

I realise how in awe I am of the young girls on the course and how the awe is tinged with envy. I must have been like them when I was young, but I thought I wasn't. How I envy their bodies, their luxuriant hair, their tans, their boyfriends, *their confidence. They have skeins of hair, waterfalls of it, pulled over one shoulder. They remind me of the Elves of Rivendell in Lord of the Rings, with their unfurrowed brows and bright clear eyes. I try not to regret missing out on everything during my youth but it is there, acknowledged. Momentarily, I wonder what growing out my grey roots will do to my sexual currency in the world. I want more than ever to stop hiding behind makeup, hair colour or anything else that masks my true self. Here I am, world.*

*I have forced myself into the midday sun. For many people this is their comfort zone, paradise even, when the sun is high and they are most likely to tan. For me, it is extremely stressful. I have to be slathered in Factor 50 because I burn so easily. I have to coat my hair in coconut oil before I get in the water to stop the colour doing something weird and I don't like stickiness or sand on my body. I am still afraid of the waves (although less so due to swimming lessons and Shubham) and I don't like how you have to repeat the cream-slathering every time you come out of the water.*

*I have spent other middays until now in my ice-cold, air-conditioned room, hiding and studying. I want to practice tapas and come out of my comfort zone. Why can't I be one of those women who just lies in the midday sun and gets in the water? Why do I worry about everything? I even start to think I've gained weight, just to add to it all. Do what needs to be done, Lisa. Stop eating all the food. As Sudhir says, "You don't need to eat everything on the menu."*

*I am at the beach outside Juliet's pink cottage but she is not there. She has flown back north. There are no dogs on the beach and it's strange. I wonder if they're being fed somewhere? I just sit here, in my bikini in the blinding white light, journalling my thoughts.*

*There is a lifeguard nearby in his red uniform and*

shades. And then, Chris appears. I love how we are never far from one another. She comes towards me, gesturing without looking at me to move over on my beach throw and she stretches out beside me. We lay next to each other and I smile. What a connection. This woman – wise, funny, beautiful – is yet another spirit guide in my Agonda journey. Everywhere I go today we cross paths, as if we are dancing.

I get up to go into the water and later, Chris tells me that she didn't know I had gone – she could still feel my presence next to her. I thought she might join me in the sea, but when I look back she has already gathered her things and is walking back along the beach. I smile.

The waves are strong today due to pre-monsoon weather and sitting in front of them, I feel baptised and renewed. I close my eyes and in my mind there is a bright, white light and I am holding my heart in my hands. I laugh when I open it up like an Easter egg and find Shubham sitting inside it, cross-legged, looking up at me. His dark eyes shine into my soul and his smile lights up my heart.

I love him.

I am finding it difficult to accept that this can actually be true. That I can be happy. I've got so much wrong in this life so far that I can scarcely believe it could ever be right.

On this beach, in the blinding white light, I cry. Such joy.

Everything seems so aligned here, so right. Maybe it was always meant to be like this. I will write and teach yoga and make a living from things that I love doing. I will be with Shubham even though he is half my age. I may not have him forever but I have him right now.

I am bursting with happiness. This is how you shine even brighter in your life – you come to a place you love, to people you love, doing a thing you love. I am so grateful to Agonda for revealing all of this to me.

*It is time to stand in the light of the future and not in the darkness of what has gone before. What was done is done and I will stop depriving myself of love and happiness, thinking I don't deserve it. It was here, all the time. Inside me.*

*Evening time and we meditate with Sudhir. He asks us to consider the gentle moon overhead. In my mind, I can see tiny brave turtles in the moonlight, launching themselves into giant waves that carry them gently to their new lives. In my mind, I can see Shubham's ship sailing back to me.*

*I can't wait to get to bed so that I can wake up the next morning and tell Chris the decisions I've made. I can't wait to tell Shubham that I love him.*

*I am awake at 5am and the wifi is still off.*

*It will have to wait.*

---

I went back to live in Agonda for six months as a freelance editor and writer in November 2019. I completed more yoga-teacher training and I even started teaching drop-in classes at Sampoorna and wrote the school's online blog. I was 'living the dream', as they say. I rented rooms in a big red house near the sea owned by a local Catholic family and spent Christmas with them. Shubham returned from his cruise ship just in time for New Year – our anniversary.

In late January, I took a trip to Rajasthan for the Jaipur Literature Festival where I attended a session on memoir-writing: Elizabeth Gilbert was on the panel. It was my first time in the 'real' India and I was surprised at what I saw. Not at the horror and hassle everywhere that I'd been told to expect, but at how wonderful it was.

I hired a tuktuk driver for the week and he took me for chai and curry after my first day at the fair. I spent most of my time laughing – at his videogame driving, with the people in the tuktuks next to me, and at the animals criss-crossing our path. It was like being on a fairground ride. I loved Jaipur, the pink city, and the haveli I stayed in, its walls covered in bold madhubani paintings of Hindu gods and goddesses.

Afterwards, I travelled on the train via Pushkar to Udaipur. The experience was nothing like the one described by friends, who'd told me about stinking toilets and people packed into small cars. I paid for a standard seat on a standard train and sat with mainly commuters on their way to work. Men selling chai, pizzas and SIM cards wandered down the aisles. It was madly normal, but for the distressed state of the train, with its worn leather seats and faded blue paintwork.

In Rajasthan, I noticed that Indians allow things (and people) to age in a way that we don't in the West. We constantly upgrade, modernise and replace. All I saw around me were repurposed materials – oil drums as seats outside chai bars for one – and painted doors allowed to peel and fade in the sun. They looked beautiful. I liked that almost nothing was new and decided that when I got home, I wouldn't be so prepared to replace everything I owned all the time.

I fell completely in love with Udaipur. It felt like an Indian Venice with its bridges, lakes and winding medieval streets filled with life. I planned to go back and live there for a few months during the next season while Shubham was on his ship.

But then coronavirus reared its ugly head. I'd dismissed it from the comfort of my Agonda bubble, where no one was taking it seriously. It was just another virus, just like flu. But the news had started to scare me and I started looking at leaving a month early to come back to the UK. Flights were starting to be cancelled and I worried about getting out.

For a week or so I thought I could live in Agonda for the monsoon and weather out the COVID crisis there. Surely my friends there would look after me if things got tough. That's when two good friends, Kay and Paula, staged an intervention, saying that the Indian healthcare system would flounder in the crisis. I couldn't risk catching coronavirus there.

"GET OUT OF INDIA NOW," Kay's husband wrote as his email subject, when I wouldn't listen to his wife's exhortations. I'm slightly ashamed to say I listened to the man. (As it turned out, Goa would be fine for another year, but the Delta variant of the virus eventually arrived in 2021 and floored India's healthcare system.)

Two weeks before I left Agonda, Shubham surprised me with a birthday cake. It had my name in icing on it and a small lit candle. I cried at the gesture. The cake had flopped a bit from being carried on his Enfield but I didn't care. Here was someone who cared about me enough to bring me a surprise cake on my birthday.

I knew it would be the last time I saw Goa – and Shubham – for a long time, so I made the most of those last days. I memorised every step we took in the sand, every smile he flashed me, and the feel of my arms around him as we whizzed around beaches on his bike. I can still recall every detail, including the texture of his skin on the morning I said goodbye. Leaving him, my friends, the dogs, felt like having my heart cut out. The day before, I'd had another bout of uncontrollable crying. I knew that my emotional response showed how deeply connected I was to the country and to the man.

# WORTHING BEACH

## WEST SUSSEX, ENGLAND – MARCH 2020

I BREATHED IN THE FRESH, cold air on Worthing promenade, so good after those hot and humid pre-monsoon months in India. I walked along the beach wearing a warm coat, carrying a flask of hot tea. I chatted to people at a two-metre distance and said hello to all their dogs, getting used to seeing them wearing collars and leads again. I looked at all the painted stones left on benches by children and marvelled at the bubbled whelk-egg cases blowing around like sea-blossom. Daffodils were in bloom that reminded me of Wales and there were noisy crows everywhere behind the rows of beach huts. They reminded me of Agonda.

The highlight of my walk was a Second World War 'pillbox' in Ferring that gave me a view over the beach down to the sea. It was a concrete platform edged with a bird-filled hedge and benches. The benches were studded with plaques containing messages to deceased loved ones. The path leading up to it through Goring-by-Sea was made of blinding white limestone. When the tide was in, the ocean reminded me of the aquamarine necklace I'd bought in Jaipur – a sparkling, soft green.

Standing looking out towards France on the pillbox, I could see a wind farm, its blades slowly turning like children's seaside windmills. Out west I could see the white tented structure of Bognor Regis Butlin's, the shimmering headland of Selsey Bill, and in the distance behind them, the shadowy bulk of the Isle of Wight.

I'd chat to birdwatchers with binoculars who'd tell me what they'd seen that morning. One day, it was a pod of dolphins and I borrowed their (sanitised) binoculars and saw them too. The birdwatchers told me that it was migration time, so it was a good time to see birds flying from all corners of the world. If the wind was right, they hugged the English coastline, if not, French birdwatchers would see them instead.

On the pillbox, people I didn't know would suddenly share their stories with me and I'd never see them again. One woman was struggling with her husband's lockdown anxiety. She cried. I couldn't hug her.

I made friends at Sea Lane Café in Goring-by-Sea, where the owners welcomed me in as their first lockdown customer. I quickly became part of the Sea Lane framily, making a stop for tea and toast part of my daily routine, meeting my new socially distanced friends, a couple both called Tony. I frequented the Cloud 9 Coffee blue horsebox on the prom; a chat with owner Dave while I waited for my coconut cappuccino quickly became the only way to start my day.

My London flat was still being rented out so I was renting rooms from Elsa and Dave in an Edwardian house near the sea. They had a ten-year-old son called Finn, a lurcher called Nerys and a Bengal cat called Bob. We all became firm friends. I was trying to replicate my Agonda living experience here in the UK, walking by the sea every morning before working at the kitchen table during the day and then walking again in the evenings.

Although leaving Goa had been a wrench, moving to Worthing for lockdown turned out to be a good choice. I loved the town with its stony beach and fresh white pier; the pier was studded with stained-glass panels that reflected coloured light onto its wooden decking. Out on the end of it in the evenings, I'd see flocks of starlings in murmation over my head.

Worthing people were friendly. We smiled at each other on the prom, relieved to be by the sea during lockdown, away from any corona chaos in the cities. They reminded me of people in North Wales, eager for a chat. My old self willingly obliged. I met up with people I'd been friends with in Brighton in the nineties. It felt as though a circle was completing.

In my freelance work, I began to find new creative joy in helping individual authors make the books they'd written in lockdown the best they could be. For much of my career, I'd taken an inflated salary for flouncing around in meetings, and dealing with sociopaths and narcissists. I'd been nowhere near actual books for years; I'd been surrounded by PowerPoint decks and Excel spreadsheets. Now, I found working closely with authors hugely rewarding and I loved the feeling of earning an honest buck. I edited a book – I got paid for it. I was writing too. I was doubly happy on half the income and for the first time in my life, I managed to save money.

I chose who I wanted to work with and set boundaries around my time and availability. I worked the hours I wanted to work and that was most likely to be 11am until 7pm. If it was going to rain on a Saturday, I took the day off on the Friday and worked the next day instead. If I wanted to go to somewhere else to hike (COVID-allowing), I could up and go without having to book time off. I had the ultimate working freedom, there at the kitchen table. I got a couple of calls about publisher jobs in London. "No thank you," I said, knowing what I'd be giving up.

By autumn 2020 I'd realised I wouldn't be going back to India for the dry season, so I moved out of my shared lodgings and rented a flat of my own with its own garden not far from the sea. I hung up the strings of mirrors I'd brought back with me from Agonda. They reflected the light from the sea into my rooms.

I learned during all three lockdowns that I love being on my own. It truly makes me happy. I'd always thought that the purpose of my solo wandering was to find what was missing in my life. But now I'd discovered what had been missing: me. I loved the silence and found that I was completely happy with my own thoughts. I didn't need music, radio, podcasts or audiobooks to accompany me anywhere, as I had in London.

I hiked on the South Downs with my friend Paula at the weekends, but in spring 2021 I started doing solo walks, using an app to navigate. All I needed was a small Jack Russell and I'd be back again in full Brontë mode, as I'd been as a girl in Wales, roaming about on the moors alone. Walking was a way for me to process everything. Every morning, I'd think about work I'd done or work to come, reflecting on ideas and solutions to problems. I thought about what I wanted from my new life and who I wanted in it. By the time I got home I'd have a list of ideas and plans typed into the notes app on my phone.

I managed to stay away from the prosecco in the supermarket and I started cooking for myself rather than relying on ready-prepared things. I simply hadn't taken care of myself at all in my former life and now things were changing. I taught yoga on Zoom for a small group of friends, and did my own regular practice. There was no doubt about it: lockdown was one of the happiest times of my life.

During one of our many videocalls during the first lockdown in 2020, I told Shubham that one of our friends had told me I should let him go. "There are plenty more fish in the sea," he'd said. "After all, he's 26!"

Shubham seethed when I mentioned it. "I only want you," he growled.

The feeling was mutual.

Shubham also had people questioning my intentions with regard to him – European people he worked with in Agonda, supposedly 'looking out' for him. They couldn't believe that we might actually be in a relationship. And we weren't, technically, but this was a bond that didn't need a name.

But other people's comments about us made me wonder if I was damaging Shubham's chances in life by holding on to him. He could find a nice Indian girl and have a family, and not waste his time on me. Maybe lockdown was the universe telling us to separate for good. We'd had our moment together but we weren't meant to be – I should do the right thing and let him go, even though I knew it would kill me to see him with anyone else.

In summer 2020, a guy I'd met on a hike asked me out. I told Shubham about him and he surprised me with his response. He kept his composure. He said that all he wanted was for me to be happy, and that if I'd found someone better than him, then he was happy for me. I told him that I hadn't found someone better, just someone who could offer me a future. Shubham wasn't able to offer me that and he couldn't deny it. He had 'responsibilities' to his family, he said, with tears in his eyes.

So I began dating the hiking guy, as much as you could in between the first two lockdowns. My friends seemed happier with the situation – I was finally 'sorted out' with an age-appropriate man; he was forty-eight. They liked to remind me that my 'relationship' with Shubham could never go anywhere, because of his age and his culture. He'd be expected to marry a nice Goan girl and have babies. They encouraged me to properly end things with Shubham so that we could both move on.

I know they said those things because they cared. And I knew they were probably right. But I was unhappy with the suitable man. I could only think about Shubham the whole time I was with him and I was still carrying Shubham with me in my heart. I was still speaking to him regularly and he kept telling me that he only wanted me to be happy.

And then it became apparent that the suitable man had given me false hope about what he was offering. He invited me on week-long hiking trips away, but then announced he wanted to 'take things slow'. It was obvious that he was only really interested in me as a hiking fuckbuddy, his lockdown entertainment. I had suspected as much at the start, but ignored the red flags because I wanted so much to be 'sorted', to fit in. And I wanted to blot out my real feelings for Shubham with something – someone – new and exciting.

But this guy reminded me too much of Dean. He had the same charm and chat, that flirtatiousness with everyone he met. And then, on a beach in Northumberland on one of our hiking trips, I'd turned around and seen him giving me that same lascivious look. I couldn't believe I'd fallen for it again.

When I revealed that I was single, Shubham told me

he'd been heartbroken by my near-desertion but tried to hide it. I'd tried to set him free by entering a new relationship, but he'd waited for me. He knew I'd be back. I now knew that we had a bond that couldn't be broken, but we were separated by the coronavirus and a third lockdown; there was no hope of me getting back to India, or him onto a cruise ship.

And then he finally got the call. Shubham would be coming to the UK in April 2021 via Heathrow, and joining his ship in Torbay. Surely there would be a moment where I could see him, fleetingly, from two metres away? But we were thwarted at every turn. We found out that he would be bundled onto a coach as quickly as possible at the airport and put into a hotel to quarantine. I found myself delivering a care package to Novotel staff and standing outside while a smoked-out window was opened slightly and a set of brown fingers wriggled into the gap.

It was him! He'd been six thousand miles away and now he was here. Finally.

I adjusted my position in the hotel car park and saw a flash of his gap-toothed grin and his black hair through the gap in the window. I tried to work out what he was shouting to me without resorting to using my phone. And then I heard it clearly.

"You're my fish!"

---

I don't know why, but after the third lockdown in 2021, I felt compelled to visit a medium. I wanted to see if it was possible to connect with my long-dead parents and find out what they thought about me and my life.

I found Miriam – a psychic – who lived and worked on

Worthing seafront in a spacious period home with comfy leather sofas and shelves of books.

She saged the room as I sat down, chattering from the moment I met her, making small assessments about me that were entirely correct, looking into my depths with her sparkling brown eyes. She was a beautiful fortysomething German woman with high cheekbones and long, shiny brown hair.

She identified Shubham straight away. "I see a dark-haired, tanned young man who could be your son!"

We laughed about the age gap. I told her that Shubham was currently going round and round the UK on board a cruise ship, unable to get off, orbiting me like some sort of moon. Miriam told me we had a very strong connection.

Of course, I already knew that – our bond was like a gravitational pull. As long as we were in each other's orbit, it didn't matter that we weren't in the same hemisphere, country or town. We'd spent three years like this and our bond was getting stronger in spite of our physical separation. Miriam told me that the distance between us was serving a purpose, allowing me to spend time on my own.

I asked her if my parents were there and she described them as they were when I was born and told me how they had both died. There were details that she couldn't have known from a google search.

"They're holding a book..." she said.

I knew it had to be my book.

This one. The book I'd laid aside because people kept telling me I shouldn't publish it.

"*People won't like you,*" they said. I'd already lost a friendship.

"*You've written it too quickly – memoirs take at least two years,*" they said. I'd taken two months.

*"You should turn it into fiction,"* they said. I wanted to write the truth.

*"You can write something else!"* they said. But I wanted to write this book.

And then there were friends who said the opposite...

*"It's amazingly honest and that's a rare commodity,"* they said.

*"People who have reacted adversely to it are probably unable to face their own fears,"* they said.

*"You are living a life that women aren't supposed to live,"* they said, *"and this is absolutely why you need to get it out there."*

I knew that what I'd written the first time around was a confessional, almost an act of self-flagellation. I'd poured everything out and it was riddled with guilt, bitterness and anger ... and blame. I had spent a lot of time blaming others for what had happened to me, but I had been the agent of my life and I need to accept responsibility for it. I had the freedom to choose how to respond to what had happened.

I'd lived with regret for far too long and had finally started to see my life as simply a journey to where I was now. Nothing had been wasted. I'd made a set of choices that were right for me at the time, and I'd learned from them and moved on. I needed to look at my story again, clear-eyed and sober, and tell the truth.

"Oh that's strange... Why are they showing me that?" said Miriam, suddenly and sharply. "Your parents are showing me fire. I can see pages in it."

My brain went into a frenzy. Should I be burning the pages of my book?

Miriam reassured me that it didn't necessarily mean that I had to burn anything. It could relate to a burning passion. It could refer to the burning of the old and the rising of the new. A fresh start.

A transformation.

I suddenly had the clarity I needed. I walked home, smiling in the sea air, knowing I was going to get this book out again and rework it for self-publication under my real name, not a pseudonym as originally planned. The text had already undergone around four major revisions, and the process had been a form of therapy. For a while I thought that was what the book's purpose was – to help me. Miriam thought differently.

"You're here to help people," Miriam had said, passing on a message from my parents. "You're on the right path."

*Do what needs to be done, Lisa.*

I would flood my story with the light of everything I'd learned and take the darkness out of it. If my story helped other people to realise that they could make different choices, that they had options, it would be worth it. If it helped them to give up drinking, see a relationship more clearly, and stop criticising their bodies, it would be worth it. If it gave them the confidence to make a leap into the unknown, it would be worth it.

I'd stand in the fire and burn.

# MORFA BYCHAN BEACH

## LLYN PENINSULA, NORTH WALES – JULY 2021

*I have reached my destination. Time to remove my hiking boots and feel the hard ripples of the exposed sand at low tide under my feet.*

*The wide strand of the beach is flooded with sunlight. No North Welsh grey lid.*

*I am at Morfa Bychan – Black Rock Sands. The last time I was here was the early eighties. I stayed in a caravan behind the dunes with my mother and our Jack Russell, Sherry. The holiday park is still here.*

*I can see Sherry bolting off, running around the beach in a huge loop, unable to contain herself in this new and exciting environment.*

*My mother is saturated with sadness, missing her husband. She hasn't made friends with anyone at the caravan park. She has come here so that the dog and I can run free on a beach. She remembers doing the same thing herself, in her younger days.*

*I feel Mum's hand in mine as I walk, and I smile. She's here, putting one tentative bare foot in front of the other, right by my side.*

Then she turns to look at me, laughter in her eyes. "Smashing for the beach, love."

# GAYATRI MANTRA

Sanskrit, origin: Rig Veda, c.1500 BCE:

*Om bhur bhuvah svah*
*Tat savitur varenyam*
*Bhargo devasya dhimahi*
*Dhiyo yo nah prachodayat*

English translation by Douglas Brooks:

*The eternal, earth, air, heaven*
*That glory, that resplendence of the sun*
*May we contemplate the brilliance of that*
    *light*
*May the sun inspire our minds.*

## ACKNOWLEDGMENTS

Thank you to all the friends and publishing people who read the early drafts of this book and were so helpful with their feedback: Jenny Heller, Elv Moody, Sally Morgan, Sam Missingham, Julia Kingsford, Chelsea Berlin, Tobias Steed, Angela Elkins and Aruna Khanzada.

Thank you to Katherine Halligan for buying me a copy of the life-changing *Eat, Pray Love* and Justine Solomons for telling me I was clever and I should write. Women don't say that to each other enough. Thank you to Clare Baggaley for designing the beautiful cover, making me stick with this title, and for all her creative support.

Thank you to Kay Woodward and Helen Peacock for caring when I was on holiday in Thailand alone that first time. And thank you to Kay and Andrew Woodward and Paula Newton for 'encouraging' me to leave India just before lockdown. I found it terribly hard, but you were right...

There are many guardian angels I've encountered along my journey, from Thai women on motorbikes to removal women. I didn't know it at the time, but they formed an invisible chain of female support for me, when I thought I was alone. Thank you, ladies.

Thank you to the Simrose team in Goa – especially Dinesh, Manish, Ajay, Malika and Saroj – for keeping me going with coffee, masala chai, lime soda and 'crispy toast' as I wrote the first draft, and to Sweetpea for lying supportively at my feet.

And the Kopi Desa boys: Shubham 1, Ram, Shubham 2, Manoj, Anup and Shushant, for endless lime sodas, hummus and pitta bread, and chat.

Thank you to Deepak Sharma and Eli Aguilar at Sampoorna Yoga School in Agonda and yogis Sudhir Rishi, Veena Sudhir, Lucia D'Angelo, Karen Marsh, Christine Horton, Agnes Jarosch, Alexandra Van Schaik, Karma Joy, Ida, Sally Wooldridge, Emily Lacy and Danni Cullen for helping me see the world as it really is. Thank you to Gita Thakur for the many breakfast dresses and chats.

Thank you to Peter and Gavin at Sea Lane Café in Worthing and Cloud 9 Coffee Dave, for keeping me supplied with take-away drinks during all the lockdowns and the various redrafts of this book. Thank you to Elsa and Marzi for opening your homes to me during lockdown.

Thank you to George, Gary Bebb of Go London and Paula Newton for showing me what adventure looks like and enabling me to find the wild places.

Thank you to authors Elizabeth Gilbert, Cheryl Strayed, Raynor Winn, Alastair Humphreys and Robert Macfarlane for showing me which paths to take, and to Annie Grace and William Porter for telling me the truth about alcohol. Thank you to Jean Kelly for telling me to read Annie's book.

Thank you to Dr Vanja Orlans for releasing Little Lisa, and to Miriam Pfeil for allowing her to talk to her parents.

Thank you to Mum and Dad for showing Miriam this book and for always being in my life even after death. It's all for you.

And finally, thank you, my darling Shubham, for your encouragement as I poured these words out, and your offer to help me publish them in India.

That's when I knew you were my fish.

# ABOUT THE AUTHOR

Lisa Edwards is a former publisher who is now a freelance writer, editor, agent and yoga teacher. She grew up in North Wales, but has lived mostly in southeast England. She lives in Worthing, West Sussex, where she walks by the sea every day. She splits her time between the UK and India.

facebook.com/becauseyoucan50

twitter.com/Redwoods1

instagram.com/redwoods1

linkedin.com/in/lisa-edwards-34991115

amazon.com/author/lisa_edwards

ALSO BY LISA EDWARDS

Because You Can – one woman's guide to living without alcohol

Because You Can Blog